Building Inclusivity

Making your workplace Equitable, Diverse and Inclusive

Toby Mildon

R^ethink

Contents

Introduction   1

  Achieving a cultural shift   3

  My story   5

  How this book will help   8

1 Awareness: Embracing The Conversation And
  Reaching A Common Understanding   11

  Defining equity, diversity and inclusion   11

  Misconceptions of equity, diversity and
  inclusion   16

  The importance of equity, diversity and
  inclusion to business   20

  Demystifying and normalising equity,
  diversity and inclusion   23

  What to raise awareness of   26

  How to raise awareness   30

  Developing empathy   32

  Summary   34

2 Engage: Leadership's Role In Championing Equity, Diversity And Inclusion   **37**

Why you need the senior leadership team on board   38

What prevents engagement?   39

Rogers Diffusion Curve   44

How to speak to the senior leadership team   46

Understanding the journey   48

Psychological safety   51

The Five Dysfunctions of a Team   54

Summary   57

3 Beyond Tokenism: Leadership's Role In Cultivating Inclusive Cultures   **59**

Getting clear on the why   60

Developing inclusive leadership skills   65

Working with your employee networks   68

Committing to the plan   69

Summary   71

4 Analyse   **73**

Analysis and the employee experience   73

Communication and overcoming concerns   78

Ways of gathering data   82

Doing it right and GDPR   84

You're good to go   88

Summary   91

5 Interpreting Equity, Diversity And Inclusion Insights **93**

Workforce demographic data 95

Quantitative inclusivity data 103

Qualitative inclusivity data 104

Return on effort and investment data 105

Best practices 107

How to analyse and report on your findings 110

Artificial intelligence: The exciting future 114

Summary 114

6 Plan: Strategising For Equity, Diversity And Inclusion Success **115**

Gap analysis and benchmarking 116

Go back to the why, how, what 122

KPIs and targets 125

Formulate the strategy 126

Summary 130

7 Implement **131**

Change management models 132

Roadmap to underpin your strategy 140

Summary 143

8 Improve And Sustain Change: From Strategy To Action **145**

Adaptability and responsiveness 146

Putting Agile into practice 147

Sprints, capacity and empowered teams   149

The Game Changer Index   151

A business strategy for continuous
improvement   154

Continuous support and guidance   158

Celebrating success and positive PR   161

Summary   162

Conclusion   **165**

Appendix   **167**

Scorecard   167

Notes   **171**

Acknowledgements   **177**

The Author   **179**

Introduction

If you are the head of HR or chief people officer for your organisation, you are aware that your employees are your biggest asset. Although it is often regarded as a cliché, you genuinely believe in the idea that investing in your people and empowering your teams is key to unlocking your organisation's full potential to deliver exceptional services, create phenomenal products and make a positive impact on the world. Your employees want to work in an organisation where they feel respected and like they belong, where they are empowered to do their best work, and where they can advance in their careers. Millennials and Generation Z – our future leaders – in particular have high expectations of social justice, the environment, and the values and culture of the companies they work for.

An inclusive culture is essential not only for employees but also for the end users of your products and services. Engaged employees provide a better service or build a better product if they feel they work for an organisation that is aligned with their values and needs.

Even though you believe an inclusive culture is important from a strategic perspective, your senior leadership team (SLT) may be reluctant to embrace it. They may be unaware that a lack of equity, diversity and inclusion (EDI) is causing issues for the organisation. They may not appreciate the value EDI adds to the business, or they may not have seen any evidence that it leads to greater profitability. EDI may not be a high-priority issue or strategic differentiator for them. External forces – like a slowdown in the economy, geopolitical uncertainty, generative AI, cybersecurity threats, climate change regulations and changes in consumer behaviour – are more pressing or urgent for them in the shorter term, as are strategic imperatives such as mergers and acquisitions to grow the business, and IT transformation initiatives to reduce costs and increase efficiency.

You may lack the data to convince them of the importance of EDI and to build your business case. A lack of data, or fragmented data, prevents you from giving them a deeper understanding of what problems employees encounter in real time so that they know the challenges the organisation faces. To drive change, you can use data to build a sense of urgency. Without the information, how can you create targeted solutions that make an impact where it matters, with a good return on investment (ROI)? Data changes EDI from being a soft issue to impacting the bottom line of a business.

Achieving a cultural shift

All of this leaves you frustrated and overwhelmed because you know something needs to be done, but where do you begin? You want to feel a true sense of accomplishment in your own role and make a tangible and positive difference in the lives of others in your organisation. In spite of the inequalities in today's society, you want to be confident that your business is creating equitable opportunities for people to gain meaningful employment. Without the necessary support, how can you realise the necessary cultural shift?

In the absence of a cultural shift, people will leave the organisation if they feel disrespected or that they don't belong or aren't valued, to go and work somewhere that is more aligned with their values and meets their individual needs. You know employee turnover is expensive. Productivity during the recruitment process declines. You use up other people's time, pay for recruitment tools (such as assessments) and suppliers (which includes agency fees and training costs). Mistakes happen as new employees learn the ropes, and there is a cultural impact too. Line managers are stressed and distracted when they have to keep recruiting and replacing people, which is a real cost to the business.

The worst thing is that if a lack of EDI persists, then the business is at risk of damaging its reputation and becoming irrelevant in the market. Clients will go where they can find a diverse workforce that reflects themselves. If you do not invest in an inclusive culture and meet the needs of top industry talent, that talent will not want to work for you. A lack of diverse perspectives, colleagues from similar backgrounds and co-workers with similar educational and career experiences may also lead to groupthink and stifle innovation.

You need a practical strategy, a roadmap, to guide you on how to implement an EDI cultural shift – a strategy that is integrated with the organisation's vision, mission and strategic objectives and is integral to its success rather than being just something the HR department does to the organisation. As a result, EDI becomes a part of the organisation's DNA in a sustainable way. Employees feel valued and respected, and want to continue working for you. The creation of this inclusive culture will help your organisation grow, innovate, remain relevant and be future-proofed. It will make it easier to attract diverse talent.

There are many resources and a lot of information about EDI already; why should you listen to me? Google 'diversity' and 'inclusion strategy' and you'll get 773 million results. One day, I asked ChatGPT to create a diversity and inclusion strategy, and it took only 212 seconds for me to get one, but using an AI-generated strategy that isn't tailored to your unique organisation or trawling through millions of Google responses is not recommended.

My story

I have lived experience of both inclusion and exclusion within the workplace. Although I was born with a rare genetic neuromuscular disability (spinal muscular atrophy), which means I am a wheelchair user and require twenty-four-hour care, I have always had a strong work ethic. EDI is important to me because I have experienced inclusive, supportive behaviour from managers and allyship to help me reach my full potential and thrive in the workplace.

I've also been on the receiving end of discriminatory and prejudicial behaviour, which adversely affected my self-esteem and mental wellbeing and prevented me from achieving my full potential. Since disabled people have often been portrayed negatively in society, and unhelpful stereotypes and implicit biases emerge as a result, people frequently have low expectations of disabled folk. I'm also gay and my teenage years were filled with shame. I felt I had to prove myself more than my nondisabled peer group.

I wrote to several companies to request work experience but got rejected until I made an appointment with the manager at Lloyds Bank to open a savings account. At the end of the appointment, he asked if I needed anything else. I said, 'Yes, actually, could I get a job please?' To my surprise, he arranged for me to work for the bank, and I worked there on and off during my school, college and university holidays for three years or so. He was the first inclusive manager I encountered: he saw my disability but he also saw my potential and became my ally and sponsor. Due to having Lloyds Bank on my CV, I got jobs at British Airways, Accenture, Cerner, the BBC and Deloitte. To this day, I am grateful for this manager, as I do not know where my career would have gone without his support.

Later in my career, I had a less positive experience while working on a client site. The client's health and safety manager toured the building and told me I was a fire hazard in my electric wheelchair and that I should leave the building immediately. I did so, but after a while I did not want to be separated from my team any longer, so I returned to the office despite the client not being able to arrange an appropriate fire evacuation procedure for me. After being kicked out again, I cried in the disabled toilet. I sent an email to the client that included the F-word and was then hauled into HR, where I was told off for upsetting one of our top-tier clients. In hindsight, I realise this was a 'career limiting move', but at the time I felt like I wasn't given enough support by my employer. This incident forced me to leave and work elsewhere.

After working for the BBC for a number of years, I felt proud that, even though I am disabled, I could work for one of the world's most prestigious and respected broadcasters. It was through my work at the BBC that I was able to develop many opportunities (despite having started in technology). For example, I helped get Liz Carr cast as Clarissa in *Silent Witness*, a drama that is widely considered to portray disability well. I worked in the newsroom during the Olympic and Paralympic Games of 2012 and also advised on accessibility of the Tardis and set for the Doctor Who Experience.

After they had asked me to implement our action plan to attract and recruit more women into technology roles in our design and engineering department, the BBC allowed me to switch career paths from IT project management to EDI. Initially, it was a part-time position, but I quickly realised it was a full-time role and that I needed to consider diversity in its broadest sense rather than just in terms of gender balance. The BBC had been my home for a decade, but I wanted to return to the corporate sector. I joined Deloitte, who were committed to establishing an inclusive and respectful culture.

Now, I am a consultant who provides inclusivity expertise to companies with typically more than 250 employees, including Centrica, Sony Pictures, Xodus Group, Okarno (part of the larger Saint-Gobain Group) and Turley. My portfolio also includes boutique businesses, such as an Agile consulting, training and coaching company with twelve employees and a founder who is interested in company culture as the business scales.

How this book will help

When I wrote my first book, *Inclusive Growth*,[1] which outlines clear, accessible and actionable principles to make a lasting, positive difference on inclusivity at work, I wanted to share best practices with other organisations and advise them on what they should focus on when implementing EDI in a genuine, authentic, sustainable way. This second book builds on that information and explains how EDI strategies should be designed and implemented in an organisation from beginning to end. Having worked with clients over the years, I know how overwhelmed you may feel when embarking on your EDI journey and not knowing where to begin with developing your strategy. I created the Inclusivity Flywheel as a model for developing and implementing EDI changes in your organisation in a sustainable way. What is a flywheel? A flywheel is a rotating wheel that stores kinetic energy. Flywheels generate more energy as they rotate, building sustainable growth that's easier to scale than pushing a traditional linear process uphill.

My Inclusivity Flywheel model incorporates learnings and best practices from my clients as well as from my own mistakes in the past. It comprises five segments:

1. **Awareness** – to raise awareness and normalise EDI in the workplace

2. **Engage** – to engage your senior leaders in creating the right climate for change

3. **Assess and plan** – to enable organisational evolution and develop your strategy

4. **Implement** – to put your inclusion ideas into practice in a way that makes an impact

5. **Improve** – to ensure ongoing support and long-term guidance

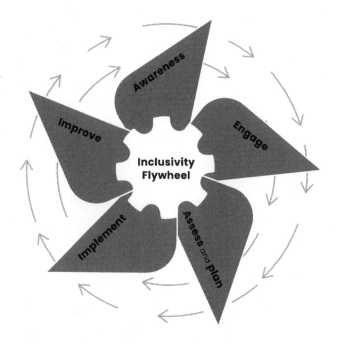

Using the Flywheel model, you can become a champion and catalyst for promoting EDI within your organisation by gaining a deeper understanding of each of these key topics and more. The impact this has on your organisation's culture will make you a trailblazer, and you will leave a lasting impact.

ONE

Awareness

Embracing The Conversation And Reaching A Common Understanding

Awareness is the first step of the Inclusivity Flywheel model, and in this chapter we will look at how you can raise awareness of EDI in the workplace. We will define what EDI means, look at the language of EDI and deal with the common misconceptions that surround EDI.

Defining equity, diversity and inclusion

When you begin your EDI journey, it's important to be clear about what it means to your organisation, your SLT and to you personally. This also applies to organisations that are well into implementing their EDI strategy but are not satisfied with its progress and are considering a reset. There is often confusion around EDI terminology. Some companies talk about diversity and inclusion. Others switch it around to inclusion and diversity, with reason (focusing on a culture of inclusion, which will attract and retain a diverse workforce, is often seen as preferable to putting diversity and our differences at the forefront). Some include equality, equity, respect, belonging or justice.

What do these terms mean, and how can we simplify them for our colleagues working on the shop floor who don't think about EDI as part of their role?

Whenever I begin my Diversity Includes Everyone workshop, I introduce the iceberg model.[2] In this model, 10% of the iceberg is poking above the waterline. This represents our visible or apparent characteristics, some of which are enshrined in equality legislation (for instance, the Equality Act 2010 in the UK or the EU Equal Treatment Directive). The remaining 90% of the iceberg is hidden beneath the waterline. This represents our invisible, or non-apparent, characteristics, which we often don't consider as part of our diversity dimensions. For example, being an introvert or extrovert, whether you grew up in the countryside (like me) or the city, whether you are from a military family and travelled a lot as a consequence, as well as the more traditional characteristics such as an invisible disability (like dyslexia) or being a member of the LGBTQIA+ community but not being open at work about your sexuality.

Given these non-apparent characteristics, we need to appreciate just how broad our diversity is and that, in fact, diversity includes everyone because we are all different and unique in some way or another.

Unfortunately, a lot of organisations take a hierarchical approach to EDI. They focus on one particular group of people or characteristic at a time; for example, they might concentrate on women in leadership or women in technology and engineering because there is particular under-representation in that part of the business and the science, technology, engineering and mathematics industries. Or they might create an annual plan focusing this year on gender, next year on race and ethnicity, mindfulness the following year and disability the year after that. Consequently, in this instance, your disabled colleagues are left feeling unseen, unheard and undervalued.

By taking this rather siloed approach, intersectionality is completely overlooked. By that I mean the combination of different social and political identities and lived experiences that give us overlapping inequalities in the workplace. My personal experience as a white disabled gay man who grew up in the West Country is different from a friend of mine who has the same disability but is British Indian, born and raised in London by parents who both worked as doctors. Even though we share similar characteristics (spinal muscular atrophy, an ambitious personality, a warped sense of humour), we have different ethnicities, grew up in different parts of the country, and come from different social classes. As a result, our experiences in the workplace have been different, and we have both experienced different types of discrimination and inequalities throughout our working careers.

When we talk about diversity, it is important to think about representation. Are our businesses representative of the cities in which they are located, the communities and clients we serve, the talent pools we draw from and our clients' diversity? Across the UK, this can vary a great deal. My client in the Nottinghamshire countryside has access to a different talent pool to work in their distribution centre than another client headquartered in Birmingham. If we aren't representative of the diverse talent in our towns and cities, then what is going on in the recruitment process that prevents people from getting through and receiving a job offer? Companies' relevant industries can affect their talent pools, especially those that require university qualifications. This is a real challenge for such companies, or, perhaps more concerningly, a perceived challenge that allows companies to claim it is the industry's fault.

Once you understand that diversity is about representation, you need to shift the conversation towards equity and inclusion because, although you may have a diverse workforce, some people may not feel included, respected or like they belong and are empowered within it. You can also have a homogeneous workforce where everyone feels included because they come from similar backgrounds but you fall into groupthink, which limits innovation and creativity and creates areas of weakness within decision-making.

To shift the conversation towards inclusion, we need to keep these four considerations in mind:

1. Does the organisation give people a sense of **belonging**?

2. Are people **respected** for who they are? Can they bring as much of themselves to work as they like?

3. How **empowered** do people feel, particularly in relation to their manager?

4. When working for you, will people be able to **progress** in their careers?[3]

Why do we need belonging and respect? Belonging is about feeling part of a group, being included and connected to others within the organisation. Respect, on the other hand, is about valuing and acknowledging individuals for who they are, including their identities, backgrounds and viewpoints.

Misconceptions of equity, diversity and inclusion

Since EDI has become an industry in itself, several misconceptions and poor practices have developed over time. Here are some of the most common:

- **EDI begins and ends with particular groups of people.** For example, a business might focus on gender rather than consider the broad spectrum of identities and lived experiences.

- **Diversity is binary and you are either diverse or not.** I called my training programme Diversity Includes Everyone because I wanted to stress that we are all diverse and unique.

- **EDI is not the responsibility of those who don't identify as being diverse.** Some people think that because they're not, for example, a woman, disabled, gay or from an ethnic minority background that EDI doesn't apply to them. If we want to create an inclusive culture, then everyone has to share responsibility within the workplace.

- **EDI is just a tick-box exercise.** This does happen in some organisations where they run lots of superficial initiatives. Some companies, for example, will change the colour of their logo during LGBTQIA+ Pride Month to say that they are a wonderful LGBTQIA+-friendly organisation. This view is not always supported by LGBTQIA+ employees who work there.

- **Diversity is about filling quotas or hitting targets.** This often drives the wrong behaviours. Most worrying is that it particularly affects certain individuals. For example, if there's a target to get more women onto the board and a woman gets appointed to a board position, she might wonder whether she was the best person for the job or was selected to meet a target. There is also much confusion between quotas and targets. If you don't hit a quota, then there can be consequences like not getting your bonus. A target is an aspirational goal; if you don't hit it, it's not the end of the world, but it's something to aim for. Aiming to meet targets and quotas can often lead to driving the wrong behaviours; however, setting specific, measurable goals is important, and we'll be covering that later in the book because, as Peter Drucker once said, 'What gets measured, gets managed.'[4] If you are not setting measurable objectives or targets about how representative you want your workplace to be, then you are unlikely to achieve your goals.

- **It is only minority groups who benefit from EDI.** We all benefit from working in an equitable, diverse and inclusive organisation. You may make something accessible for a disabled employee, but you will probably improve the usability of a workspace, system or process that will benefit everyone. For example, flexible working arrangements, first introduced to accommodate a disabled employee's commuting challenges, offer extensive benefits when applied organisation-wide. This inclusive policy improves the work–life balance for all employees, including those with caregiving responsibilities, increases productivity and expands the recruitment pool by removing geographical barriers. It also reduces environmental impact by cutting down on daily commutes and has the potential to lower operational costs through reduced need for physical office space, benefiting the organisation as a whole.

- **It is the HR department's responsibility to promote EDI.** EDI is everyone's responsibility. Although the HR department does hold the lion's share because it's often about the 'people' agenda, other departments are also accountable. Marketing needs to consider how inclusive and representative their marketing campaigns are. The procurement department needs to think about how diverse the supply chain is and whether they're working with minority-owned businesses to boost the economy. The IT department should ensure that their systems are accessible. Facilities management needs to think about whether the building is accessible and whether you have things like gender-neutral toilets.

- **EDI is just a fad.** In reality, EDI has been around for a long time. The history of EDI dates back to at least the mid-twentieth century, with formal efforts beginning in response to legal changes and societal demands for equality. It has since evolved, incorporating the concept of equity and adapting to the changing needs and challenges of a diverse world.

- **Organising training and creating employee networks or employee resource groups (ERGs) is all you need to do.** These initiatives only scratch the surface. You must develop a well-thought-out, longer-term, sustainable approach to achieving EDI. This is something I talk about in my first book by setting out seven best practices: clarity, culture, change, colleague experience and design, cyber, collaboration and celebration).

- **Inclusion means that everyone agrees.** That's not the point of inclusion. Inclusion is about ensuring that we welcome, listen to and acknowledge people coming from different backgrounds, with different lived experiences, different opinions and ideas. It is OK to disagree with one another as long as we create an environment of trust, respect and constructive debate.

The importance of equity, diversity and inclusion to business

It is important to highlight the key reasons why EDI is so important. In my talks and webinars, I often run a poll to find out why EDI is important to various businesses. In order of popularity, here are a few reasons that managers commonly mention:

1. You can attract and recruit people more easily because your organisation becomes an attractive place to work.

2. You retain employees for longer. Every time someone leaves your business, it costs you money. You have to re-recruit, and you have the cost of a person who may not be performing as they prepare to leave. Then there's the cost of training a new person to get them up to speed.

3. You avoid groupthink, and you are more innovative and creative. If you have a homogeneous team, everyone thinks along the same lines.

4. You minimise exposure to legal risk. For example, somebody may take you to tribunal if they feel they have been discriminated against. Tribunals are time-consuming, costly and damage your reputation. Think of the damaging headlines about sexual harassment at McDonald's and at Uber (costing Uber at least

US$4.4 million), the 'culture of fear' at BrewDog or H&M facing several controversies related to racism and insensitivity in its advertising and products.[5,6,7,8]

5. Your decision-making is more effective. As Erik Larson argues in his article in *Forbes*, diverse teams make better decisions because they bring different perspectives and experiences and they can see around areas of ignorance.[9]

In terms of financial performance, McKinsey's research consistently shows that companies with more diverse workforces tend to perform better financially. Several McKinsey reports, including *Diversity Matters Even More*, *Diversity Wins*, *Delivering Through Diversity* and *Why Diversity Matters*, have reinforced this link.[10,11,12,13]

While some business leaders may struggle to relate the popular McKinsey reports to their organisation, there are many other reports, papers and books from reputable authors and institutions emphasising the business case. One of my favourite books is *The Difference: How the power of diversity creates better groups, firms, schools and societies* by Scott Page, professor of complex systems, political science and economics at the University of Michigan.[14] It is a favourite because the author shares evidence that the benefits from diversity and inclusion can be demonstrated statistically. He argues it's not just

a social justice imperative but a crucial ingredient
for enhancing creativity, problem-solving and
innovation, which can only benefit businesses.
He challenges the reader to think of diversity and
inclusion beyond fairness/ethics and really delves
into the benefits of generating robust, innovative and
adaptive solutions.

Peter Cheese, the chief executive of the Chartered
Institute of Personnel and Development, told me in
the 'Diversity and inclusion as the golden thread'
episode of my podcast interview, The Inclusive
Growth Show, that HR professionals need to speak
business language and be commercially minded to
succeed. Often, we fail to take this into account when
we talk about EDI.[15]

It is a good exercise to check whether EDI ties
in to your organisation's values. At the BBC, for
example, we had a value that said 'We respect each
other, we are kind, and we champion inclusivity.'
In another example, TomboyX has the value:
'Diversity: we champion diversity and inclusion;
everyone is welcome and appreciated. We celebrate
our differences, foster a sense of belonging, and
show our commitment through our words and
actions.'[16] This is further supported by accountability,
fearlessness, trust and unity. The direct link to EDI in
these examples is clear. Other businesses will have
something similar, but they might also have values
that are implicit and indirectly linked. For example,

my favourite BBC value was 'We collaborate, learn, and grow together.' While this doesn't mention EDI specifically, working collaboratively is an inclusive leadership trait, as is building relationships and having a growth mindset, so there is an implicit link to that particular value. By linking values, you are helping people to see how your existing values relate to the EDI topic.

Demystifying and normalising equity, diversity and inclusion

A whole industry has been developed around EDI, with its own language and acronyms. Some of the terminology you might hear is accessibility, allyship, belonging, bias, cultural competence, culture fit, cultural intelligence, diversity and inclusion (or inclusion and diversity), equity and equality, ERGs, intersectionality, justice, microaggressions, micro-inequities, micro-incivilities, microculturalism, neurodiversity, privilege, power, the patriarchy, stereotype threat, tokenism, under-representation and visible minorities. It's multifaceted. It gets even more interesting as you navigate historical barriers and cultural dynamics. For example, there is a whole history around racial inequality and racism, gender equality and disability rights. People feel overwhelmed not only by the history and its ripple effect on inequalities in our society today but also by the right language or wrong language to be using. In your role as an EDI professional, it is your responsibility to simplify the topic and make it more understandable.

Empathy and an open mindset are key characteristics of an inclusive leader. It's also about being courageous enough to ask questions and connect with new people and ideas. People are often worried about saying the wrong thing and causing offence. When you challenge yourself, when you go beyond your comfort zone, you may discover that you have your own biases. It's possible that you have said or done things in the past that may have been considered disrespectful or insensitive (I certainly have) even if you didn't intend to offend anyone. The importance of apologising, learning from the experience and continuing as allies cannot be overstated.

Now that we have talked about what EDI is and some misconceptions around EDI, we need to normalise it. In this sense, EDI should be an OK topic to discuss so that we can appreciate and celebrate our differences and cultures; for example, organising an event during Ramadan to raise awareness of the Islamic faith. In the end, we want to appreciate, understand and celebrate our differences and see them as a strength rather than a threat.

A term often used in work is 'bring your whole self to work', which means everyone must be respected.

Ultimately, you need to create an environment where people feel comfortable being themselves at work. Because not everyone wants to be open at work about being in a same-sex relationship or living with a non-apparent disability, I prefer to use the phrase 'bring as much of yourself as you like'. Having an open environment will allow people to talk about themselves as much as they want to without feeling ashamed about their uniqueness.

The right environment will give people the confidence to address inappropriate behaviour and start to 'call out' or 'call in' that behaviour. Calling out is being able to say in real time what you notice and challenge it. For example, you might notice that a male colleague keeps interrupting or talking over a female colleague during a meeting and you raise it with them in the moment. This might be to prevent further harm or send a signal to the wider meeting. Calling in might happen after the meeting, when you take someone to one side for deeper discussion, reflection and understanding.

A useful framework for addressing inappropriate behaviours is Purple Flag Moments, in which you identify offensive words and behaviours.[17] You respond by observing and naming offensive words and actions, asking the question 'What makes you think that?' or 'Can you elaborate on your point?' Another approach is reframing the conversation. My experience has taught me that challenging people in this way can be awkward. How do you respond without being defensive if you have been called out for insensitive behaviour? It's important that you don't create a climate of fear around making mistakes. Take a breath and pause. Thank the person who shared with you for their feedback. Commit to improving and ask questions to learn. This is also an opportunity to let people know how problems can be escalated.

Some companies have speak-up tools where anonymous feedback can be given through an app, or an employee assistance programme (EAP) that people can access, or there might be an ethics or whistleblowing hotline that can be used to raise awareness, making this a good opportunity to let people know how poor behaviour can be flagged or raised.

What to raise awareness of

A crucial step in developing your EDI strategy is to raise awareness. You can raise awareness of many different things; however, the following is a list of suggested topics:

- Different aspects of diversity dimensions and lived experiences – for example, gender and gender identity, menopause, LGBTQIA+, disability, race and ethnicity, mental health, religion and beliefs and other lived experiences

- Rights movements and their history – for example, the disability rights movement and the history of disability rights

- Unconscious bias – for example, a similarity bias when a manager prefers hiring a candidate with a similar educational or career background to themselves

- Microaggressions – the small behaviours that are disrespectful and undermine us, for example, repeatedly mispronouncing someone's name or talking over somebody in a meeting

- Privilege and power dynamics – for example, the structural, disciplinary, interpersonal and hegemonic power dynamics devised by Patricia Hill Collins in her matrix of domination, which identifies four key power dynamics and are crucial to understand and address if we are to create a truly inclusive and equitable workplace environment:

  - Structural power, which shapes organisational policies and hierarchies

  - Disciplinary power, involving the enforcement of workplace norms and behaviours

  - Interpersonal power, seen in day-to-day interactions and relationships among colleagues, potentially manifesting as bias or discrimination

- – Hegemonic power, which reflects the overarching cultural norms and values within the organisation that may implicitly favour certain groups over others[18]

- Legislation, such as the Equality Act 2010 in the UK, the Americans with Disabilities Act of 1990 or the EU Equal Treatment Directive

- Making reasonable adjustments (or 'workplace adjustments' as I prefer to say)

- The business case of EDI

- How to be an effective ally

- Being an active bystander

- Inclusive leadership skills

- Inclusive communications and accessibility

- How to give feedback

Raising awareness and educating people about EDI is crucial not only to build an inclusive workplace but also to avoid efforts that are overwhelming and drain resources with little impact. To ensure effectiveness, conducting a comprehensive learning needs assessment is vital.

To conduct an EDI learning needs assessment, you should follow these steps:

1. **Identify goals**: Define what EDI means for your organisation. Establish clear goals for what you want to achieve in terms of knowledge, skills and competencies.

2. **Survey employees**: Collect information from employees through surveys or interviews. Ask about their current understanding and experiences, and if there are areas where they feel more training is needed. Don't focus just on under-represented groups in your organisation but have a survey that covers everyone including leaders at all levels.

3. **Analyse existing training**: Review any existing EDI training programmes. Determine whether they are meeting the needs of the organisation or there are gaps.

4. **Identify gaps**: Compare the information gathered from the surveys with your goals. Identify areas where employees' skills or knowledge are lacking.

5. **Plan training**: Develop a training plan that addresses these gaps. Ensure that the training is relevant, engaging and accessible to all employees.

6. **Implement and evaluate**: Roll out the training and regularly evaluate its effectiveness. Seek feedback from employees and make adjustments as needed.

How to raise awareness

There are lots of ways in which you can raise awareness. Here are some suggestions:

Events and speaking

- Acknowledge international days, eg the UN International Women's Day or the UN International Day of Persons with Disabilities

Hold events and workshops

- Attend conferences and then share your learning with colleagues

- Arrange for external speakers to visit your organisation

- Invite celebrity speakers with lived experience, such as Ruby Wax or Stephen Fry, to give an insight into mental health

- Organise art exhibitions showcasing artists from diverse backgrounds

Training

- Offer live training sessions with external trainers – face-to-face or online

- Incorporate Train the Trainer programmes by using EDI experts to create a training programme and then training your own trainers or employees on how to deliver the programme, thereby increasing your internal capability

– Use online training videos and e-learning – these can either be pre-made or you can commission an agency to make content for you

Digital media

– Use social media, eg LinkedIn

– Communicate internally using platforms like Microsoft Teams and Slack

– Conduct surveys and polls

– Share information through newsletters, blogs and articles

Traditional media

– Share your message through print media such as posters, flyers, brochures and booklets

Partnerships

– Work with local community groups or charities

Once you have created your learning needs assessment, you will be able to determine which of the activities above meet your learning needs. Identify what you can realistically do, otherwise you may feel overwhelmed by all that you could do and get frustrated about not making an impact. You may end up repelling people rather than engaging them if your campaign lacks authenticity and meaningfulness.

Developing empathy

Empathy is the ability to recognise, understand and share the thoughts and feelings of another person. It involves both cognitive understanding and emotional connection. As Stephen Covey says in his book *The 7 Habits of Highly Effective People*, 'Seek first to understand, then to be understood.'[19]

The importance of developing empathy as a key skill is further endorsed by Catalyst in their report *Words Aren't Enough: The risk of performative policies*.[20] The report was written at the height of the global pandemic and in the wake of the murder of George Floyd at the hands of police brutality in the US. In addition to dealing with a global pandemic, business leaders were figuring out how to support Black colleagues after George Floyd was murdered, how to become anti-racist organisations and how to protect employees' wellbeing. Catalyst found that if organisations had a genuine and authentic response to racism within the workplace and during the pandemic, then there were significant benefits in terms of employees managing work–life demands, feeling respected and valued, being engaged, planning on staying in the business and experiencing greater inclusion. When I interviewed Dr Tara Van Bommel, senior director and statistician at Catalyst, on my podcast, she said, 'We found that the presence of genuine policies and senior leader empathy was key to decreasing burnout, which refers to the feelings of overwhelming emotional exhaustion, cynicism and a diminished sense of efficacy at work.'[21]

The report identified empathy as the number one skill leaders and managers need to develop, so it is imperative to prioritise empathy within the workplace. Later in the book, in the Perceptions model, we will discuss five other key behaviours of an inclusive leader at any leadership level in your organisation.

CASE STUDY: Medical Protection Society

Medical Protection Society (MPS) is the world's leading member-owned, not-for-profit protection organisation for medical and dental professionals, supporting nearly 300,000 members globally. Despite significant internal EDI advancements, including an EDI forum and various inclusive networks, MPS opted to intensify these efforts. Rather than a conventional workshop format, MPS collaborated with my team for a Train the Trainer approach.

Andrew Myers, an in-house leadership consultant at MPS, explained, 'Our aim was not to restrict EDI as merely an HR initiative. Since managers play a pivotal role in hiring and promotions, it was paramount they were the primary participants.'

We introduced our Diversity Includes Everyone programme to selected MPS employees. This training decoded diversity, emphasising the importance of mirroring the communities MPS engages with. An interactive survey revealed different perceptions of inclusivity among colleagues. The course deeply explored unconscious bias, privilege and microaggressions, rounding off with how EDI integrates with MPS's values and growth strategies.

After selecting the trainers, we conducted two sessions for them to observe. These sessions culminated in a live 'best practices' guide, which MPS adopted for future use. As a result of this approach, training slots were filled quickly upon announcement and feedback was overwhelmingly positive.

Summary

In this chapter, you have seen that raising awareness is the first step towards building an inclusive workplace, but it isn't sufficient. You are only scratching the surface. As part of building an inclusive organisational culture, you need to change your behaviours.

In many organisations, training objectives and expectations are often unrealistic. For example, when it comes to unconscious bias training, you need to remember that as humans we have a lifetime of ingrained implicit biases because of the way our brains are wired and the effects of social conditioning, which cannot be undone in a two-hour masterclass or in a mandatory hour-long online training module that most people resent logging onto. At this stage, you must be realistic about your objectives.

EDI needs to be talked about more openly and frequently to make it less of a taboo subject. For sustainable inclusion strategies to be developed, you must first raise awareness, get people comfortable talking about EDI matters, and then shift behaviours. You also need to link back to your organisational values and ensure that you're living and breathing them and walking the talk. Your goal should be to create an environment where people can be proud to share their differences and uniqueness and feel able to share more about themselves.

TWO

Engage

Leadership's Role In Championing Equity, Diversity And Inclusion

A successful EDI strategy depends on the engagement of your SLT, which is the second step of the Inclusivity Flywheel model. Without their involvement, driving your strategy forward will prove difficult. In this chapter, we will explore why the SLT are important to EDI, as well as why they may not engage with you. We will also discuss how you can build the SLT's confidence to engage in EDI and, ultimately, how you can engage them.

Why you need the senior leadership team on board

SLTs are the custodians of an organisation's culture. People subconsciously tell themselves they don't belong in an organisation if they cannot see themselves reflected in the SLT. Because of this, they don't put themselves forward for promotions or they might even leave the organisation. It is crucial that the SLT model the inclusive behaviours you want to see in your organisation and are on board with EDI, because you need that top-down strategic direction. Many organisations take a bottom-up approach, establishing ERGs or employee networks to raise awareness and organise events. While this creates a groundswell, their activities still need to be aligned with the business's strategy and centralised EDI plans. As the SLT are responsible for strategy development across the business, it is their responsibility to ensure that the financial, commercial, marketing and people strategies encompass EDI.

When considering their business strategy, many organisations take account of the three Ps of the triple bottom line – People, Planet and Profit.[22] They want to contribute to and make a positive impact on the sustainability agenda. They want to increase inclusivity and reduce inequities for their community and create an equal and inclusive workplace for their people. Yes, they want to make a profit, but they want to do so in a responsible, ethical and sustainable way. Because of this, it is essential that efforts around EDI are linked to the organisation's 'good growth' strategy, vision, mission and purpose.

What prevents engagement?

According to Brené Brown, leadership vulnerability is 'uncertainty, risk, and emotional exposure. It's that unstable feeling we get when we step out of our comfort zone or do something that forces us to loosen control.'[23] In my experience working with many senior leaders and chief executives, fear is a key reason why senior leaders don't engage fully in EDI. They are afraid of using language that might cause offence or embarrassment. They are afraid of being 'cancelled' for saying something inappropriate, even though that was never their intention. Often this fear leads to inaction. Leaders don't lean into their vulnerabilities. They don't have difficult and awkward conversations. They don't go into curiosity mode or a growth mindset. They freeze and this inaction prevents an organisation from taking the bold steps needed to create an inclusive culture.

Biases and oversight can also hinder the SLT. As human beings, we have our own implicit biases. This is, in part, due to the way our brains are designed and wired. It is also the result of the impact of social conditioning or priming that we are exposed to – how we are influenced by TV, the media and books we read, and role models like parents and teachers, celebrities or people high up in business or politics.

As an inclusive leader, you must be aware of your biases and accept that it is a natural human phenomenon to have them. Don't beat yourself up about it but learn how your biases impact your perceptions and decision-making, which could have a downstream impact on the inclusivity of people around you. A useful framework to further your understanding is the NeuroLeadership Institute's SEEDS Model, which sets out five groupings of biases that are common in the workplace.[24] These are:

S **Similarity bias:** We prefer what is like us over what is different. We therefore subconsciously create in-groups and out-groups. We then over-appreciate the skills and experiences of people inside the in-group while overlooking or undermining the skills, experiences and abilities of those in the out-group. A common similarity bias is that we more readily 'click with' those who went to the same university as us or have had a similar career background to us.

E **Expedience bias:** This occurs when we are under pressure to meet deadlines or when we have a high cognitive load. We are more likely to take shortcuts. We act quickly rather take our time. An example of expedience bias is going to the same person on the team to get a job done because we know that they can do it quickly, with minimal supervision, and make a good job of it; however, there might be somebody else on the team who would benefit from working on that task. This bias exposes us to risk because if the person we depend on to do the job leaves, there will be a skills shortage.

E **Experience bias:** This occurs when we take our perceptions to be the objective truth. My favourite saying to explain this is that 'we falsely think that we accurately see the world, and then we make decisions based on what we falsely think is true' (otherwise known as confirmation bias). For example, if a colleague says, 'That's just the way that we do things around here,' or 'I tried that ten years ago. It didn't work. We won't be doing that again,' we know that experience bias is kicking in. Experience bias appears regularly in creative and problem-solving situations, limiting creative thinking because we revert to what we know works well or the way that things are normally done. Inclusive leaders are fantastic at challenging the status quo.

D **Distance bias:** This happens when we prefer what's closest to us to what's far away in time and space. This bias can be found in distributed or remote teams, or organisations with offices around the world. This bias can occur online, too, where we prefer someone who is quicker to answer our emails or messages than others. Another example is the difference between candidates meeting us face to face and online for a job interview.

S **Safety bias:** This is found when we prefer to protect ourselves from the downside rather than seek out the gain. As human beings, we tend to play it safe to protect ourselves. This is how our brains are wired. While this is a good mechanism to protect our human race, it's not always helpful in the workplace. For example, when dealing with a project that is failing, that has cost a lot of money and time, we suffer from the 'sunk cost fallacy' and we tend to put in even more effort, money and time to salvage it, whereas the best thing might be to quit and cut our losses.

Most available unconscious bias training is about our biases in favour of or against different groups of people. This is something we can determine by taking the Harvard Implicit Association test.[25] I took this test and discovered that I am mildly biased against disabled people, which is interesting given that I was born with my disability, my brother has the same condition, I went to school with disabled kids, I've worked with many disabled adults and I have several disabled friends. The question is, now that I have that awareness, are there any unintended consequences? Does this bias affect my decision-making when I interact with another disabled person? Will I give them the benefit of the doubt if I'm interviewing them or promoting them? Am I going to have higher or lower expectations of them if I'm line-managing them?

It's important, after taking the test, that if you do have a bias, you don't mislabel yourself as homophobic, racist, misogynistic, sexist or ableist etc. That's not the case, because our biases are normal. We can be influenced cognitively (how we think) by our cultures and experiences, which can lead to stereotyping. We can be impacted affectively (how we feel), which can lead to prejudice. Culture and experience can also influence us behaviourally (what we do), leading to discrimination. Change on a cognitive level is much harder than being aware of what we do and changing our behaviour. SEEDS allows us to focus on how bias affects decision-making and choices, ultimately affecting inclusivity.

Imposter syndrome is another barrier to senior leaders getting involved in EDI initiatives. In many cases, senior leaders either do not think they are diverse enough or believe they don't have the right to discuss particular issues because they don't identify with certain characteristics. I conducted an EDI survey for a Fintech company and found that everyone except LGBTQIA+ employees felt like they belonged. I discussed the results with one of the organisation's directors, who said, 'But who am I, as a straight bloke, to talk about LGBTQIA+ matters?' Following our conversation, he realised that he had a responsibility as a senior leader to talk about these issues so that LGBTQIA+ employees felt heard and noticed and he could champion change that would make LGBTQIA+ employees feel more included in the organisation.

Senior leaders often feel that they should know all the answers and need to be seen as though they know what they're doing. This puts them under a lot of pressure.

The last point that prevents the SLT from engaging is the perception of time and effort. Many leaders feel that EDI is something they need to add to their role that requires additional effort. It is more about doing things differently, showing up with different leadership qualities, acting as an ally and removing obstacles for employees.

Rogers Diffusion Curve

The Rogers Diffusion Curve is a model used by companies when releasing new products to market; however, it is also an excellent model to use when introducing a strategy for EDI in an organisation.[26] It is portrayed as a bell curve. The left side represents 16% of your audience. These are the innovators and early adopters who can't wait to get involved. They totally get EDI and, like people who camp outside the Apple store for the latest iPhone, they can't wait to get involved.

Once you've engaged with the early adopters, you then create a tipping point at which you can bring on the early majority (and then the late majority) of people in your organisation. This represents 68% at the middle of the bell curve. On the right-hand side of the bell curve are the remaining 16%, who are the laggards. They might never get involved in EDI.

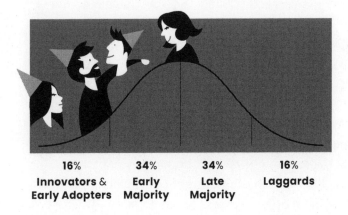

16%	34%	34%	16%
Innovators & **Early Adopters**	**Early Majority**	**Late Majority**	**Laggards**

This model demonstrates that you don't have to appeal to everybody. You need to identify your initial audience and start working with them, and the majority of people will follow with confidence. There will always be those people who won't get involved. This might mean that, later down the line, you have a difficult conversation with your board about whether those who don't align with the values of the business and raise the bar on your company culture are the right people to have in your organisation.

How to speak to the senior leadership team

There are two key ways in which senior leaders can think – logically and emotionally. Logical and rational thinkers are interested in facts and figures. They will want to know the numbers behind the business case. It is likely that they have read the McKinsey reports discussed in Chapter One and are aware of the positive impact that a diverse workforce can have on the financial performance of the company.

A senior leader who is an emotional thinker may be passionate about EDI or have a personal connection to it. They might be the only openly gay director on the board. Their child might be autistic. They may just be people-oriented, or what we might refer to as 'playmakers', and value building relationships with people or consensus within teams.[27]

I share this oversimplified psyche of a senior leader because you need to understand the person you are talking to and use their language if you are to engage them fully in the EDI conversation. To get a logical rational leader onside, you need to show them employee engagement data and put a logical business case together for them, ensuring you have all the appropriate facts and figures at your fingertips. If you are working with an emotional thinker, tell them personal stories of people in the organisation and how they are affected by a lack of inclusivity. Remember to take into consideration the 'big red dot' that we all have in between the rational and emotional sides of the psyche. This red dot contains our fear, vulnerabilities, implicit biases, imposter syndrome and ego.

As a person working in HR, you need to understand the difference between logical and emotional thinking and get curious about what's going on for that individual in their unconscious mind. I find it helpful to use the Six Thinking Hats model by Edward de Bono when talking to senior leaders about EDI, to reframe the subject in five key ways and facilitate a more effective discussion.[28] The five coloured hats represent the following different ways of looking at issues:

1. The white hat is about **facts**. With this person you need to present data and evidence.

2. The yellow hat represents **optimism**, or **the upside**. In this case, give information that shows how EDI benefits the organisation. Explain how you will attract and retain talent because you have created a more engaging workplace.

3. The black hat connects with **risks, difficulties** and **problems**. Here you need to show the impact of not being inclusive – eg not being inclusive could create behaviours that mean the organisation ends up in a costly employment tribunal resulting in reputational damage to the business.

4. The red hat represents **feelings** and **emotions**. Here you want to paint a picture of your vision of how people might feel in the organisation. Do you want to give them a sense of belonging? Do you want them to feel empowered and proud to work for the organisation because of its values?

5. The green hat represents **creativity**, **possibility**, **alternatives** and **new ideas**. Blue-sky thinking is essential in this case. Present people with innovative ideas that other organisations aren't doing.

You may notice that I've only detailed five hats above, and that is because the sixth hat, the blue hat, is about the person who manages this thinking process (this could be you in this case). This is the person who ensures that everybody gets heard.

Understanding the journey

Many organisations focus on increasing diversity within their workplace, but they don't realise that diversity is not where it starts; it's where it ends. It's the goal. If you get your strategy right, you will become even more diverse because you will attract and retain diverse talent within the organisation.

You start your journey with equity, since it involves recognising that people have different circumstances and allocating the exact resources and opportunities needed to reach an equal outcome. Equity acknowledges that due to systemic inequality, biases and historical disadvantages, different people might need different types of support to have access to the same opportunities.

Many think that equality is where we should begin; however, this doesn't create a level playing field until we have created equity. Equality refers to treating everyone the same way for fairness, providing the same resources, opportunities and treatment to all individuals. The idea is that everyone benefits from the same support. This approach assumes that everyone starts from the same place and needs the same assistance.

To succeed, you must know the difference between equity and equality. It can be a fundamental shift in mindset for HR professionals trained to treat everyone equally and avoid anyone claiming to have been treated unfairly or differently. To be successful in creating an inclusive culture as an HR leader, you must change your mindset towards equity for you and your team.

Equality

Equity

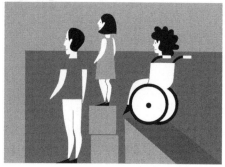

Taking myself as an example, because of my disability I can't use my hands and arms; therefore, if I am given a standard issue laptop upon joining your organisation, I will be at a disadvantage because I can't use a normal keyboard. If, however, the company installs Dragon Naturally Speaking, which is speech-to-text software, on my laptop, I can write documents and emails more quickly than anyone else. The equity created by the provision of assistive technology allows me to work alongside my colleagues, and the act of providing the adjustment helps to create equality within the workplace.

Only when you've created equity and equality, and understand the difference, can you then give people a sense of belonging and inclusion, making it easier to attract, recruit and retain a diverse workforce.

Psychological safety

An individual feels psychologically safe when they can speak up, admit their mistakes or offer up new ideas without fear of negative consequences to their self-image, career or status.

Psychological safety is important for building an inclusive culture in an organisation for the following reasons:

- It encourages open communication. When employees believe they can speak freely without retribution, they are more likely to share their thoughts. This leads to richer discussions, better decision-making and more innovation and creativity, which we know are the benefits of having diverse teams.

- Employees are more willing to propose new ideas, taking creative risks and exploring unconventional solutions, which drives innovation and growth.

- Employees will more readily admit mistakes and learn from them, leading to continuous improvement and improved risk management.

- It enhances employee wellbeing by reducing stress, burnout and anxiety.

- It can help attract and retain talent because people seek workplaces that respect and value their contributions.

Psychological safety ensures that all voices, especially those that are under-represented or marginalised, are heard and valued, and promotes active participation from everyone regardless of their background. This helps foster a truly inclusive culture.

Creating psychological safety is about curating both safe spaces and brave spaces.[29] Safe spaces foster openness, vulnerability and authentic communication where individuals feel secure to express themselves without fear, judgement or retaliation. In a safe space, a person is actively listened to and not only heard but encouraged to express themselves.

Brave spaces go a step further because the question is, who are we creating safe spaces for? Are we creating a safe space for a middle-aged, white, middle-class woman? Are we making it safe for her to talk about a difficult topic, like racism in the workplace? Or are we creating a safe space for people who are under-represented and marginalised to talk about their experiences within the workplace? If the safe spaces are created for the people and by the people who hold privilege and the power, they're going to be heavily biased in their favour rather than in favour of people who are under-represented or marginalised.

In brave spaces, individuals are encouraged to step outside their comfort zone, be vulnerable and challenge their own biases, beliefs and assumptions. For example, in a brave space, participants may be asked to share personal stories or experiences that challenge their previously held beliefs.

It's essential to construct empathetic environments where everyone thrives. You therefore need both brave and safe spaces. I see safe spaces as the foundations and brave spaces as the walls. Safety ensures psychological and emotional wellbeing, while bravery pushes us towards growth and deeper understanding. Safe spaces lay the foundation for trust and security, whereas brave spaces challenge us to confront our biases, engage in difficult conversations and grow as individuals and teams.

The Five Dysfunctions of a Team

The Five Dysfunctions of a Team is a model created by Patrick Lencioni, who identifies five common faults that teams face and offers solutions for overcoming them.[30] These dysfunctions, when understood and addressed, can lead to a more cohesive and effective team. The five dysfunctions form a pyramid and are, from the bottom:

1. **Absence of trust**: Team members are unwilling to be vulnerable and open about their mistakes and weaknesses, which prevents building trust within the team. High-performing teams are open and build relationships.

2. **Fear of conflict**: Teams that fear conflict are incapable of engaging in unified, passionate debate about key issues, leading to an environment where back-channel politics and personal attacks thrive. High-performing teams promote constructive disagreements.

3. **Lack of commitment**: This makes it difficult for team members to commit to decisions, creating an environment where ambiguity prevails. High-performing teams seek clarity and closure.

4. **Avoidance of accountability**: Without commitment, team members avoid holding their peers accountable for their actions and behaviours, leading to deterioration in the

quality of work. High-performing teams confront difficult issues.

5. **Inattention to results**: The ultimate dysfunction of a team is the tendency for its members to care about something other than the collective goals of the group. Here, at the top of the pyramid, inclusive leaders need to be aware of these issues when they are driving the EDI agenda. High-performing teams focus on outcomes.

In this book, we are more concerned about the first two levels – absence of trust and fear of conflict – as our starting point. You need trust and constructive disagreements to help create psychological safety and an inclusive work environment.

When team members trust each other, they feel safe to express their ideas, admit mistakes and be their authentic selves without fear of reprisal. This vulnerability-based trust is the foundation of psychological safety. When individuals trust their peers, they know that their contributions will be respected and that they won't be humiliated or rebuked for their views or mistakes. The environment encourages diverse voices to be heard, fostering inclusivity.

Radical candour is rooted in trust and is essential for an inclusive work environment. When team members trust each other, they can engage in open, unfiltered debates about ideas, not personalities. This ensures that all perspectives are considered and leads to better decision-making. It also means that issues are resolved directly and not left to fester, which can lead to larger problems down the road. Constructive conflict ensures that all voices are heard and that the best ideas, no matter where they come from, prevail.

The bottom levels of trust and radical candour are fundamental in establishing psychological safety and inclusivity: trust provides the safe foundation for open communication, while constructive conflict ensures that diverse perspectives are considered and valued.

CASE STUDY: Okarno

Okarno is a key UK construction brand distributor. With a clientele ranging from small merchants to large retailers, Okarno embarked on a transformative EDI journey, shifting from compliance to strategic integration. Following a workshop with the SLT, gaps in EDI were revealed, catalysing a unified commitment to change. An EDI vision statement was developed to include employees beyond the HR department, indicating a move towards enhancing company culture.

Employee feedback varied, but the leadership maintained its focus on making EDI a cornerstone of Okarno's culture. A comprehensive survey shed light on areas like mental health and neurodiversity, prompting immediate workplace adjustments, including Nook pod seating for neurodivergent employees and modified recruitment methods. These initiatives form part of Okarno's overarching People Plan, which integrates EDI into broader topics like career growth, learning and company culture.

With these steps, Okarno is helping to normalise EDI, ensuring that everyone embraces and champions it.

Summary

In this chapter, you have considered the importance of SLT engagement and what prevents them from getting involved in the EDI agenda. Using the Six Thinking Hats model, you have looked at ways to approach each member of the SLT so that you give them the appropriate information in a form that appeals to their way of thinking.

It is also vital that you understand where the EDI journey begins. Equity is the starting point. By ensuring that safe and brave spaces exist, you can then encourage open conversation in a place where people feel safe to show their vulnerabilities. It is only after ensuring a level playing field in the organisation that you can begin to attract and retain your diverse workforce.

THREE

Beyond Tokenism

Leadership's Role In Cultivating Inclusive Cultures

I n the previous chapter, we discussed the importance of the SLT's engagement in the EDI journey, but diversity can only thrive in an equitable and inclusive culture, which I define as one where people feel like they belong, are respected and empowered, and can ultimately progress in their careers. Those on the SLT are guardians of the organisation's culture.

In this chapter, we will delve into the Engage segment of the Inclusivity Flywheel and discuss the importance of understanding why you want a diverse organisation and which behaviours the SLT need to model to encourage employees to follow their lead.

Getting clear on the why

In his book *Start With Why*, Simon Sinek says, 'People don't buy what you do, they buy why you do it.'[31] I often modify this for my clients, saying people don't *buy into* what you do, they *buy into* why you do it. It is imperative that senior leaders understand why they are embarking on this EDI journey and how it will contribute to the success of your organisation.

Starting with why can be difficult. It requires us to tap into our feelings and emotions, which can be hard to express at times. Because of this, we tend to start by using the rational part of our brain (the neocortex, which controls our senses, spatial reasoning and analytical thinking) and focus on the what (what we do, the results of why), since this way of thinking and starting with practicalities is much easier. My experience is that organisations tend to focus on the what first (before figuring out the how – the process taken to achieve our purpose), before understanding what the why is. For instance, a company might host events for International Women's Day, but then discover that these events do not resolve the underlying inequalities within the organisation. As Sinek says, finding your why is a process of discovery rather than invention. Your why already exists in your organisation, you just have to find it.

I recommend you play the Five Whys game.[32] If you've got a toddler in your life, you'll be familiar with this game because they do it all the time. Just ask yourself 'Why?' five times, writing down your answer each time. After each answer, say to yourself, 'Yes, and why is that important?' Keep going until you answer the question five times. When you have finished, you will notice that you have reached a much deeper level of understanding than in your initial answer.

When I played this game on one of my webinars, an attendee who was the head of people development and culture for their company shared the following answers:

Me: Why is a diverse team and an inclusive culture important for the success of your agency?

Webinar attendee: I am concerned about the lack of diversity and inclusion in my workplace, which is in a male-dominated industry. There is significant under-representation of women, especially in senior leadership positions, and we need more representation from different backgrounds. Given the diverse nature of the area we operate in, I believe it's essential for the organisation to reflect this diversity. Additionally, the company is seeking a B Corp Certification where diversity is a significant factor.

Me: Yes, and why is it important to represent the diversity of your community?

Webinar attendee: I believe it's essential for us to give back to the community. It's not just about profits. This is a principle I truly stand by in my current workplace. At the end of the day, it's about being human.

Me: Yes, and why is it important to give back and be human?

Webinar attendee: I believe it's crucial to give back because not everyone has the same opportunities, whether in their work or personal life. Especially in today's digital world, that human touch, that personal connection, is vital. That's also what our leadership team stands by.

Me: Yes, and why is it important to have that human touch?

Webinar attendee: In the digital creative work that we do, I believe our product is closely linked with that human touch. When we show genuine care for the people we work with, they are often more motivated to go the extra mile, especially within our Gen Z demographic. This personal approach is essential for them. From our experience, by maintaining this human connection, we see higher engagement and productivity. It becomes a virtuous cycle.

Me: Yes, and why is it important that you increase productivity?

Webinar attendee: Ultimately, it's about the quality of the work we do. It's not just about making money. We see our business as a force for good. This means being beneficial for our employees, clients, community and even other businesses similar to ours. We believe in sharing knowledge and helping wherever we can. We're deeply committed to this approach.

Me: So, following the exercise we have just done – what are you thinking or feeling right now? What do you find interesting?

Webinar attendee: I found the process fascinating because it truly challenges you. It pushes you to dive deep and trust your gut feelings, sparking genuine insights and painting a clearer picture of the dynamics at play.

When I played the same game with another clients' SLT, they collectively came up with three reasons why they wanted to create an inclusive culture. First, they said it was just the right thing to do and that there was an ethical and moral case to it. Second, they wanted to create a culture of respect in their company, which was particularly important for them, since they are an employee-owned company and everyone has a stake in it. Third, they wanted to ensure that they reflected the diversity of the clients they serve and the communities with which they engage (as they are expert advisers in the built environment and work with a variety of stakeholders). These reasons are unique to them, which is why it's important that leaders find out what their unique reason is.

We don't need leaders who see EDI as just a box to tick; we need to reframe EDI towards growth, which can be achieved by doing the Why exercise and is why I wrote my first book, *Inclusive Growth*. There, I gave a framework to enable business leaders to understand that if you have an equitable, diverse workforce and inclusive culture, your business will grow.

Here are some examples of how others have linked EDI to growth:

- The NHS is about delivering better patient outcomes for everybody.

- A police force I worked with defined their why as improving the service for underserved members of their communities, as well as reporting positive KPIs to the government.

- The why of an electronics retailer I worked with was to sell more products online and increase sales revenue – by appealing to a diverse customer base, they felt they could increase revenue.

- A Fintech wanted to expand its market and reach a wider audience with their app.

Developing inclusive leadership skills

It follows that it is now important that leaders focus on their own inclusive leadership skills and behaviours. Since they are the custodians of the company's culture, how can they model behaviours that create the inclusive environment that you ultimately want? I work with the talent management experts at Talogy, who develop assessment tools for employees throughout the entire employee lifecycle. Perceptions is one of these tools and measures inclusive leadership behaviours.[33] Although there are other models worth mentioning, such as Deloitte's Six Signature Traits of Inclusive Leadership, the Perceptions model is the best set of inclusive leadership behaviours I've found so far.[34]

The six Perceptions leadership behaviours are:

1. **Empathy** – understanding and showing sensitivity to other people's viewpoints,

concerns and backgrounds regardless of their circumstances

2. **Relationship building** – connecting with people from a variety of backgrounds, establishing rapport and trust

3. **Learning orientation** – being open to new experiences and information while seeking to learn and develop

4. **Open-mindedness** – avoiding assumptions, presumptions and preconceptions by treating each individual and situation individually

5. **Composure** – controlling responses when faced with a challenge

6. **Flexibility** – maintaining an adaptable approach, style and behaviour and identifying solutions based on particular needs

Use the above behaviours as a checklist to measure your SLT against. What would be your score out of 10 for each behaviour? Which areas do you feel least confident in and want to invest time and energy in developing?

There are other behaviours inclusive leaders need, such as open communication, being open to feedback, believing in the EDI business case and being accountable for that business case. Senior leaders must also proactively champion diversity initiatives and get involved, becoming advocates and allies for under-represented groups. This might include acting as a sponsor, which is a powerful role.

Being a sponsor as a senior leader involves actively advocating for individuals, especially from under-represented groups, to advance within an organisation. Unlike mentorship, sponsorship leverages the senior leader's influence to open doors and recommend key opportunities. This role signals a genuine commitment to EDI, allowing senior leaders to leave a lasting impact, foster the next generation of diverse leaders and gain fresh perspectives to drive innovation. Under-represented groups are often over-mentored and under-sponsored, and, arguably, a leader who acts as a sponsor rather than a mentor is more effective. A senior man will not have had the same experience as a midcareer woman, so simply sharing his experience, what worked for him and what he did in his career may not be helpful to a woman who has worked part-time, has experienced imposter syndrome and has different values. The impact of a sponsor would be greater in this case.

These behaviours are essential in helping you identify the inclusive leaders in your organisation so that they can then become role models and mentors for others.

Working with your employee networks

It is vital that senior leaders develop a good relationship with ERGs or employee networks. ERGs are self-organised employee groups that represent people who identify with a particular characteristic – eg LGBTQIA+, disability, women in engineering, different faith groups or parent and carer networks. They help raise awareness and create a safe space for people who identify with that particular characteristic to get peer group support from one another.

I like to borrow a phrase used by the UK disability rights movement in the 1990s: 'Nothing about us without us', which means that you have to involve the people who are ultimately impacted when developing policies.[35] You must actively involve your employee networks in your EDI strategy development and implementation.

While this chapter is about top-down strategic leadership direction, the groundswell from your employee networks also needs to be strategically aligned. Ensuring that each ERG has a board-level executive sponsor and is proactive in their support is vital. They don't just show up to meetings; they open doors, they help secure the budget, they make introductions and remove any impediments that the group might face.

Each employee network requires a governance document to keep them on track and in strategic alignment with the organisation. Because they are passionate about inclusivity, they can sometimes veer off in different directions away from the core EDI mission. A governance document will prevent that from happening. It should include the name of the executive sponsor and identify the budget available, why the group exists, their vision and mission, how to attract and recruit members, how they will collaborate with other groups and across the business units and who their core audience are. The core steering committee team should be made up of the chairperson, the treasurer and a project manager as a minimum. The governance document will also include the annual activity plan listing the projects or initiatives for the year, along with the communication plan.

Committing to the plan

We have so far discussed the importance of understanding your why for EDI and of developing inclusive leadership behaviours, taking accountability and collaborating effectively with ERGs. It is essential, however, to create an evidence-based plan to ensure all of this great work is put into action. As we move forward, we will discuss how you put together such a plan, but first, you must create an organisation-wide climate of change for that plan to succeed.

Finally, you need to appreciate regional nuances, which are not limited to international companies. This requires a 'think global, act local' mentality. For example, there are vast differences between the UK and the US, the Middle East and Australia, and Europe and South America, but there are local differences even within the UK. The diversity that is available on the doorstep of a company based in Birmingham is different from that available to a company that is headquartered in Cornwall, for instance. You need to think about your global principles that are appropriate across the board and then consider how you can tweak them locally to make them relevant to local markets.

CASE STUDY: Turley

Turley, an employee-owned consultancy specialising in the built environment, is championing EDI with its Catalyst for Change initiative. Identifying key areas for enhancement, such as the gender pay gap and diversity in leadership, Turley is dedicated to proactively advancing its EDI agenda.

Chrysta Poppitt, senior director at Turley, recognises the necessity for swift and impactful evolution beyond traditional practices to meet their EDI aims. The company has initiated bespoke workshops and leadership forums focused on inclusive growth, and fosters environments where openness and honesty are paramount. These engagements address concerns such as the apprehension leaders may have about making mistakes, empowering them to embrace EDI principles fully.

Operationally, Turley has undertaken a thorough revision of its EDI strategy, ensuring it reflects the collective insights of its co-owners. This inclusive approach spans beyond gender, acknowledging the significant contributions of people from an ethnic minority background, disabled people and the LGBTQIA+ community, thus driving innovation in decision-making.

Several senior leaders have noted a significant change in their understanding of EDI and have applied their learning to their leadership approach as a result of the programme. To demonstrate Turley's commitment to EDI, the business employs a blend of immediate, noticeable 'sprints' and long-term 'marathons' for continuous cultural refinement.

Summary

To begin creating an inclusive culture, senior leaders must start with understanding their why. Only then can they create their strategy to bring about EDI and, ultimately, growth for your organisation.

Senior leaders need to ensure that they model the right behaviours across the business, as they are the guardians of that inclusive culture. Using the Perceptions inclusive leadership behaviours checklist will enable you to identify where your senior leaders are in terms of being role models and help you plan to bridge the gap.

Creating an inclusive culture is a responsibility shared by all leaders across the organisation and, to that end, you must develop an effective working relationship with the ERGs and commit wholeheartedly to supporting them in implementing their plans and ensure that they stay in alignment with the organisation's values and goals. To do this, your organisation must develop its EDI strategy.

FOUR

Analyse

Data collection and analysis are essential for the successful implementation of your EDI strategy. We will cover the topic in the next two chapters, since it is such a vast subject. In this chapter, you will learn how to collect data, how to handle the concerns people have about disclosing their personal information, and how to help them overcome these worries. We'll also explore some of the legal aspects of data collection that you should be aware of.

Analysis and the employee experience

You must adopt a comprehensive approach that extends beyond traditional demographic data to measure and understand workforce diversity. As important as it is to collect information about gender, ethnicity, disability and LGBTQIA+ identities, your focus should also include more diversity of experiences and characteristics. As a result of this broader perspective, you are not limited by only a few aspects defined by equality legislation. Quantifying the inclusiveness of your workplace culture is equally important to gain a deeper, more nuanced understanding of your organisational environment, enabling you to identify areas for improvement in both.

You must identify the real challenges within your organisation, rather than relying on assumptions about your workforce. Your budget, time and resources can be strategically allocated by accurately pinpointing these challenges through comprehensive data analysis. This approach allows you to address specific needs effectively and prevent spending time and effort on misidentified problems.

The use of data in your strategies not only solves existing problems but also fosters innovation. Data offers us new perspectives, allowing you to tackle challenges in novel ways. Incorporating data-driven innovation into your organisation can result in more effective, efficient practices, which, ultimately, has a profound and lasting impact.

Key frustrations

The analysis phase is crucial to the Inclusivity
Flywheel because it allows you to understand
what the employee experience is like and learn of
the real-world challenges people face. If you don't,
enthusiastic senior leaders might end up wasting
time, energy and money on projects or events
that don't have the desired impact. Analysis will
focus attention on what matters to people in the
organisation and prevent senior leaders sponsoring
activities that are ineffective.

When discussing data and analysis with HR heads, I
often hear several common frustrations:

- They don't have enough data. They might
  only monitor certain identities or protected
  characteristics. For example, in the UK they must
  collect data on whether somebody is male or
  female for HMRC. Now I understand that there
  are multiple gender identities, but, unfortunately,
  HMRC have not yet caught up with the times.
  Because they might not collect data on other
  characteristics or identities, they do not have
  enough data.

- Sometimes the data is not comprehensive, as it is
  fragmented and incomplete. This creates a lack of
  confidence in the analysis and conclusions drawn.

- In many organisations, the collection of data is voluntary, resulting in a low take-up of people sharing their diversity data.

- Sometimes, data is collected but then no tangible insights or actions are taken afterwards. Employees feel frustrated that they shared their information but then don't hear what the organisation has learned and, more importantly, what action was taken.

- Organisations can be sporadic in their diversity and inclusion data collection. This means that they might work with outdated data, which doesn't reflect the current state of the organisation.

- There may be concerns around bias. Sometimes when we collect data about diversity, we appeal to people who have a vested interest because they are from a minority background, for example. Because of this, they are more willing to share their data. Those who are in the majority group might not realise that diversity is about all of us and don't think they need to share their data, as they are 'not diverse enough', but, of course, we know from an earlier chapter that everyone is diverse and therefore everyone should share their information and data.

Data scarcity should not be used as an excuse for inaction; instead, use what you have and strive to improve it as you go along.

Start with the why again

In Chapter Three we discussed the importance of starting with why. Data collection is no different, as you will begin with why again to make sure you fully understand why you need to collect data. You might want to consider the following:

- Understand how your business represents the community. If you have a head office in Manchester – a diverse city – does it look like Manchester?

- Compare employee retention rates across groups.

- Examine how promotion rates differ between groups.

- Study pay equity, pay gaps or participation in training and career development. For example, do disabled employees access training and career development programmes equally?

- Look at how inclusive your benefits are.

- Find patterns or trends in discrimination cases, bullying, harassment, victimisation or people leaving the company.

Meeting targets or filling quotas

I'm frequently asked if we collect data to meet targets or fill quotas. The terms are often misunderstood. A target is an aspirational goal set within a specific time frame to achieve a certain level of EDI. In general, targets are not legally enforceable and are flexible. They demonstrate an organisation's commitment to EDI and encourage the organisation to take proactive steps to increase diversity without imposing strict obligations. In contrast, quotas are fixed numbers or percentages that organisations are required to meet when hiring or recruiting members from certain backgrounds; for example, the number of people in your organisation who are disabled. Some jurisdictions around the world have legal quotas that, if not met, could result in financial penalties. They are more rigid and aimed at ensuring a minimum representation of certain groups.

Within the UK, the quota mindset can lead to resentment. For example, if somebody gets a job or gets promoted, they might think it was because they ticked the right boxes, not because they were the best person for the role. Others may also think that of them. It is more important to create an inclusive culture, create the right environment and provide continuous education to ensure that people understand why and how EDI is important.

Communication and overcoming concerns

Before you begin collecting data, you must concentrate on your communication strategy and address people's concerns. This stage takes more time than the data collection and data-crunching because it is so important.

To warm people up to the idea that you will ask for their personal information, develop a communications plan that includes answering the following questions:

- What is your target audience? You may want to segment your employees into different groups so you can give targeted, tailored messages. Your ERG members may need a different approach than your SLT.

- What is the message?

- How do you want them to feel, think and act on receiving your message?

- Who is the message coming from? There could be multiple messages from different people – eg the CEO, the head of HR, ERGs or your EAP provider. Do recipients trust the sender enough?

- When should the messages be sent? Prepare a timeline over a specific period.

- Which channels will you use to send multiple messages through? Don't rely on one email, as it may not be read. Consider using messaging apps, an intranet site or posters.

- What is your call to action? Describe this, eg to fill out a survey.

Once your plan is complete, test your messaging and campaign before you launch it to the whole company. It's surprising how often we unintentionally use the wrong terminology or forget to include something in the campaign. My advice is to test it with a diverse group of people first to avoid any biases. As an example, if you test only people of the same gender, you might include language about gender that they don't pick up on because they will have their own biases.

Be mindful of the concerns and objectives that your colleagues might have about sharing data with you. Think about the psychological safety or the lack of trust that exists in your organisation, as certain groups of people might feel more vulnerable in the workplace. For example, LGBTQIA+ employees might experience homophobic or transphobic remarks because of their sexuality and gender identity, causing them to avoid disclosing information about themselves. Many people are concerned about stigmatisation or discrimination against them if they get found out. For instance, some hide a non-apparent disability because they are afraid of negative consequences.

There can be fears around privacy and whether the data is held securely. Who will or will not see the data? How will it be used? Will it be used in an ethical and legal way? Some may be concerned that their manager will get access to the data, whereas, in reality, access may only be available to a limited number of people in the HR team. You must make that clear to people.

Communications must be delivered in your own brand and tone of voice. For example, Channel 4 created a poster for a data collection campaign they ran. The title of the poster was 'What's it got to do with you? 10 reasons why you should fill in your personal information at Channel 4'. This was entirely in the tone of Channel 4. The imagery, the iconography and the typography were completely on-brand. This extended to their FAQ document too, with statements such as:

- Big Brother is not watching you. Funny as that may seem.

- It's not about you. Really. Sorry about that.

- Come the revolution!

- Go ahead. Ask.

- Get your data right. That'll be the day.

Every organisation has its own culture, way of talking and brand. Channel 4's style would not have gone down well at Deloitte, for example, because they have a more formal and corporate communication style.

Ways of gathering data

There are many ways of gathering data. Three common ones are:

1. **In-house or outsourcing**: Although outsourcing is an expense because you are paying another company to do it for you, employees are often more comfortable disclosing data to an external third party because they know that their employer will not have access to the raw data as long as the data-sharing agreements are set up correctly. As you do not have access to the raw data, however, you cannot scrutinise the data to get a detailed analysis from it.

2. **An HR management information system**: You can collect the data using an HR management information system (HRMIS) such as Workday. The HRMIS may allow you to link diversity data to employee records. In addition to measuring diversity at specific seniority levels or business units, this can be used to measure career velocity, which is the rate at which someone progresses through the organisation, and whether there are differences between certain cohorts. People are reluctant to share data if it is attached to their personal records in HRMIS systems and diversity data is not anonymous.

3. **Stand-alone or as part of your employee engagement survey**: If you collect the data as a

stand-alone EDI survey, you can ask a lot more questions and do a deep dive. You do, however, need to be aware of survey fatigue if you do a lot of surveys in your organisation, which might mean you do not get the response rate that you want.

If you include EDI surveys on your employee engagement survey, you may not be collecting diversity demographic data as part of that. This means you cannot segment or analyse your data by different cohorts, and so you will hear the majority's viewpoint, which is that they feel included at the top level, but if you break it down into minority groups, you may get a different conclusion.

Engagement surveys usually get good responses, so they're a good place to begin gathering diversity data.

To get a well-rounded picture, you need to supplement your survey with other sources of data.

These may include:

- Focus groups
- Individual interviews, especially if people are uncomfortable talking in a group setting
- Interviewing your ERG leaders and members
- Old-school feedback boxes where people can add comments as they pass by

- Speak-up tools such as InChorus and Culture Shift where employees can record their feedback in real time

- Conversation platforms – eg Slack, Teams

Organisations are often sitting on a mountain of data already; therefore, you could do secondary analysis of data which is already in your systems. Use existing employee engagement surveys but through much more of an EDI lens, or investigate exit interview surveys, grievances and complaints, or the whistleblowing hotline for any EDI patterns or trends.

Crucially, this must not be a one-off exercise, because that would result in outdated information. Getting regular feedback ensures you can see patterns and trends over time, anticipate problems and slow down their development. In my experience, if you repeat the exercise, people become more confident each time because they get used to being asked for personal information, especially if you have a feedback loop that demonstrates you've heard, listened, understood and, importantly, acted on what they have said.

Doing it right and GDPR

Moving on to the fun bit. Now that you're doing data collection, you need to do it right. In this section I am speaking specifically about UK legislation and GDPR requirements. The information here has been gleaned from what I have learned through conversations with my clients and what I think is important. This does not constitute legal advice. You must get proper legal counsel either from your own legal team or from an external data privacy lawyer.

Let me start by saying that data privacy and protection are important because we are dealing with people's sensitive information and there are legal protections around that. To educate yourself on this, I recommend you read *Equality, Diversity And Inclusion Monitoring: A multi-country guide* by the law firm Bird & Bird.[36]

Speaking only of the UK, in the report they ask and answer four questions:

1. Is there a legal requirement to carry out equality opportunities and diversity monitoring? In the UK there is not a legal requirement.

2. Can employers actively promote diversity in the workplace? Yes, they can in the UK.

3. Are there provisions and data protection, law and diversity monitoring in the UK? Yes, there are.

4. Is a data protection impact assessment (DPIA) required when an employer carries out equal

opportunities and diversity monitoring? Yes, in the UK a DPIA is required.

There are special categories of data that come with additional protections. These include race, ethnic origin, health and sexual orientation. That is why you must be cognisant of data protection and data privacy which places more responsibilities on you. There might be some situations where employers have a legal obligation to process diversity data. For example, if you employ more than 250 people, you should report on gender pay gaps. If you're in Northern Ireland, you might need to do your annual religious belief monitoring form. If you're a public sector organisation, you may need to publish information to show compliance with the public sector equality duty under the Equality Act 2010.

Interestingly, legally the collection of diversity data doesn't have to be anonymous – individuals can be identifiable – but adhering to data protection law is essential in case the data gets into the wrong hands. If it gets exposed and goes public, it can damage trust in the organisation and seriously impact individuals. Remember that any data you collect must connect to the business need, which is a requirement under data protection legislation. Then be clear with employees about what data is being collected, for what purposes and how. You can address that in your FAQ document, as mentioned in the example of Channel 4. When you ask respondents for their personal information, it's a good idea to include a privacy statement that they can click through to provide their explicit consent.

HR needs to understand the risks involved. Be cautious about whether data might be misused in decision-making. There may be senior leaders who use the data with a 'quota mindset' as discussed earlier, which might then lead to discrimination claims.

The Information Commissioner's Office, which is the UK's data protection authority, can impose fines of up to £17.5 million or 4% of your global annual turnover, so there's a real financial risk if you get things wrong. Employees can exercise their data protection rights and request to see what data is being held about them. This can be time-consuming, or you can end up paying compensation to an employee if you breach their data protection rights and regulations.

It is, however, possible to collect diversity data and you shouldn't shy away from it, because the mission here is to build an inclusive workplace and you need insights from data to do that.

The key is to work with your legal advisers sooner rather than later and get their buy-in. Engage with other important bodies like trade unions, regulators or your ERGs. Also ensure you have an executive sponsor on your data collection mission, such as your legal counsel, chief operating officer or chief financial officer, who will have risks and KPIs on their radar.

You're good to go

Now that you've figured out all the above, you're good to go, but how do you overcome the problem of increasing uptake? Here are some ways that will help:

- Communicate your purpose clearly so that employees understand the importance of the survey and how the data will be used to improve the company. Even though in the UK the survey doesn't have to be anonymous, it's recommended you assure anonymity.

- Follow data protection advice. Assure your people that data is being collected and handled in compliance with the rules and regulations. To get a higher response rate, emphasise the importance of anonymity, since colleagues will then be less afraid to share personal information.

- Make it a simple process for people to respond to and provide their data. Don't use a system that is complicated and convoluted.

- Consider using user-friendly platforms, which means ensuring they are accessible for people with various impairments and disabilities and different levels of IT literacy.

- Think about where people are responding. Are they on the go, on their phone? Are they on a tablet in their work van? Are they in their own homes or in an open-plan office? Are they at their desk with a big monitor or a small screen? How do they feel in each of these locations?

- Engage your SLT as soon as possible. Use the cascade effect to roll out your survey and start with the most senior people. Then ask them to encourage the people underneath them to do the survey and keep cascading it down through the organisation. People will have more confidence in responding to the survey if their manager has done it, and their manager can talk to them with confidence about any concerns they might have.

- Plan your feedback mechanism. How will you let people know what you've learned and what actions you will take? This will demonstrate to people that it was worth their time investment. You might want to incentivise people if you can afford to. Incentives don't have to be financial.

- Create multiple reminders through multiple channels for the message to get across.

- Provide support if people have difficulty completing the survey or have questions not addressed in the FAQ document. This could be a dedicated individual or an email address or phone number that they can use if they have concerns.

- Seek external help because an external provider like me, who has done this numerous times with lots of different businesses, can help you avoid making mistakes which might be costly to you.

CASE STUDY: Gate One

As a digital and business transformation management consultancy, Gate One has taken steps to advance its commitment to EDI under the direction of Sonia Cochet, their chief people officer. With over 300 employees, Gate One is part of Havas, one of the world's largest global communications groups, allowing the business to draw on the broader digital, customer and communications expertise that the global group provides.

The firm holds events geared towards EDI, encouraging discussions and allyship among employees. Sonia's leadership has been vital to integrating EDI into the company's ethos.

Combined with existing Havas Group initiatives, Gate One intensified its diversity and inclusion efforts. Specific targets were established for increasing the diversity of the workforce and advancing women in leadership. Havas training helped the team to understand EDI principles and make it meaningful to Gate One.

To establish an EDI baseline, Gate One conducted an employee survey to gain insight into the firm's culture of inclusion. An EDI plan tailored to Gate One's unique needs was developed from data, and insights were collected from the survey, ensuring a culture where all employees feel valued and included. The plan was tailored across three workstreams, aiming to raise awareness and celebrate diversity at Gate One. A 'bottom-up' approach, taking the survey results into account with delegated leadership, mitigated the number one project risk: EDI is a sensitive and ever-evolving topic, where understanding differs from person to person.

Gate One's organisational culture has been profoundly changed by this approach, which embeds EDI in every aspect from recruitment to performance appraisals.

In the beginning, Gate One had just ten people engaged in the EDI team. Today, around forty individuals in the core team actively support improving the way they work, developing understanding and supporting operational changes, with an even wider network of champions and allies established to embed conversation across the business.

Summary

You have covered a lot in this chapter because there is a lot to do, and it does take time. It can take months, in fact. To keep things simple, break your data collection down into the following stages:

1. Understand why you want to collect data

2. Plan to engage your senior leaders and data protection advisers sooner rather than later

3. Plan your communications strategy

These three steps take the most time as the data collection can be done in a couple of weeks. The amount of time spent on analysis depends on the amount of data you collect, as we will discuss later in the book.

FIVE

Interpreting Equity, Diversity And Inclusion Insights

We've discussed the importance of raising awareness and engaging your employees and senior leaders, as well as the importance of using data in understanding what's going on in your organisation and what challenges it faces. We will discuss what data can be collected and how in this chapter.

This information is based on my own experience working with clients in professional services, healthcare, energy supply, the media, not-for-profit organisations, construction materials distribution, hospitality and technology, and the best practices I've learned along the way. That said, best practices are constantly changing, so it is crucial to keep up with the latest developments before collecting any data.

Your goal in this chapter is to learn how to collect comprehensive data across the spectrum of diversity, so it is quite broad. You need to collect a broad range of data, as you now know, since the diversity iceberg is broad below the surface. You shouldn't focus too much on any one particular group or characteristic.

There are four distinct groups of data you need to measure:

1. **Workforce demographic data**: For your business to be successful, you must reflect and represent the communities and clients you serve, as well as the towns and cities where you are based. You also need to ensure that you represent the diversity of talent pools within your industry.

2. **Quantitative inclusivity data**: Quantitative data allows you to see patterns, themes and trends.

3. **Qualitative inclusivity data**: Using qualitative questioning, you gain deeper insights into the business through comments and answers to open questions.

4. **Return on effort and investment data**: You will be able to build your business case to secure resources to deliver a change programme by

calculating things like employee attrition and employee Net Promoter Score (eNPS).

Workforce demographic data

Here are some factors that can be used to measure the demographics of your workforce.

Organisational details

An individual's length of service, location, type of employment, level of seniority and department or team are included in this. By examining EDI data from these perspectives, you will be able to see if there are any differences between departments. As an example, the data may identify areas of under-representation in one part of the business that don't exist in another, or that disrespectful behaviours are prevalent within a particular department or team.

Gender

According to Stonewall, gender is often expressed in terms of masculinity and femininity, is largely culturally determined and is assumed from the sex assigned at birth.[37] Gender is a complex and multifaceted concept, and it can vary across different cultures and societies. Gender is not strictly binary (male or female); it exists along a spectrum, and there is a wide range of gender identities beyond just male and female. As a minimum, you should ask if somebody identifies as a man/male or a woman/female (referred to as gender binary) or are non-binary. It's essential to include an 'I prefer to use my own term' field, as there are many different gender identities, including terms like agender (identifying as no gender), genderqueer and more. To include transgender individuals, you should also ask whether someone identifies with the gender they were assigned at birth.

Ethnicity

The ethnicity categories set out by the Office of National Statistics (ONS) were developed after extensive consultation and testing. They are appropriate in most cases, but they aren't perfect. Although most people identify with an ethnicity on this list, some do not, so, again, it is good practice to include a field for people to add 'I prefer to use my own term' if they wish to. Ethnicity has to be adapted for different jurisdictions, however. For example, it is categorised in different ways in the US, the UK and Australia.

In the US, Hispanic, Spanish and Latina origins are included, and Black ethnicity is discussed as, for example, Black and African American, whereas in the UK we speak about Black African, Black Caribbean or Black British. In Australia, ethnicity is discussed in terms of ancestry: English, Chinese, Aboriginal, Torres Strait Islander, Australian etc. You will need to tailor the list to your market as needed.

In the UK, please bear in mind that the categorisation of ethnicity in the census probably originated from a need to gather demographic data for policy-making and to understand the diverse make-up of the population. While this serves important purposes, such as informing public services, ensuring representation, and monitoring discrimination, it also raises concerns. Inappropriately handled, it can lead to stereotyping, privacy issues and the oversimplification of complex identities. The fluid and subjective nature of ethnicity makes rigid categorisation challenging. Hence, while ethnicity data is valuable for addressing the needs and rights of diverse groups, it must be managed carefully to avoid reinforcing divisions or infringing on individual privacy.

Disability

In EDI surveys, it is common to ask participants if they consider themselves to be disabled or if they have a long-term health condition. Disclosure rates of disability are, however, often low (anywhere between 1% and 5% in my experience), and reasons include:

- Fear of discrimination and judgement based on an individual's disability – concerns include how this information might affect their work, their relationships with colleagues and managers, and even their job security

- Concerns about confidentiality if people are unsure who would see their disability status and how it would be used

- A perception among some people that their conditions are not considered 'real' disabilities or are not 'bad enough' to disclose

- Feeling uncompelled to share their disability status at work – they may feel more comfortable managing their disability privately

- Wanting to be judged on their talents and skills and not on their disability and wanting to be seen primarily for their professional abilities

I have obtained useful disability data by using the Washington Group's set of questions, which adopt a functional approach that focuses on the difficulty of performing basic activities across universal domains of functioning.[38] This method identifies a range of difficulties, from 'None' and 'Some' to 'A lot' and 'Cannot do it at all', within six key domains: seeing, hearing, walking, cognition, self-care and communication. The aim is to understand how environmental barriers in the workplace might affect participation for disabled people.

Our approach follows the Social Model of Disability, which is favoured by many disabled people, by identifying and removing the barriers that disabled people face in the workplace. The Medical Model of Disability views disability as a problem with an individual caused by disease, trauma or other health conditions and is aimed at treating or curing them. It is an individualistic or deficit model. Conversely, the social model, which emerged in the 1970s and 1980s as a result of disabled people's activism, holds that disability arises from societal barriers, not individual impairments. Disability can be reduced and inclusivity promoted if society adapts to include all individuals, regardless of their differences. There is a growing understanding that disability is more than just a medical issue; it is also a matter of societal attitudes and structures.

The Washington Group's questions don't, however, adequately address neurodiversity, an important consideration in modern workplaces. It is recommendable to include a question about neurodivergence, such as living with autism, dyslexia, ADHD, dyspraxia, dyscalculia, Tourette syndrome or a learning disability.

You should delve further into how somebody's disability or long-term health condition affects them at work by asking about the difficulty of performing certain tasks, whether work schedules and tasks have been adjusted, and whether the workplace has been adapted accordingly. This can highlight how well the organisation is implementing reasonable adjustments under the Equality Act 2010.

It is also beneficial to inquire about mental health and wellbeing. Questions about the frequency and intensity of feelings like anxiety and depression can provide insights into the mental health landscape of the workforce. Since questions about mental health can be sensitive and triggering, it's crucial to include information about available mental health resources, such as EAPs or external organisations like Mind or Samaritans.

Sexual orientation

Stonewall defines sexual orientation as a person's sexual attraction to other people, or lack thereof.[39] Along with romantic orientation, this forms a person's orientation identity. At a minimum, ask whether someone identifies as being a gay man, a gay woman or lesbian, bisexual, heterosexual or straight. Remember to use an 'I prefer to use my own term' field here as well.

It can feel uncomfortable collecting data about sexual orientation, but it's important to note that heterosexual people are in the majority and are seldom forced to come out repeatedly at work due to their sexual orientation. In contrast, LGBTQIA+ people may feel under pressure if passing comments include 'Are you married?' and to a man 'What does your wife do?' or 'Where does your husband work?' to a woman. As a result, the individual might not disclose they are in a same-sex relationship, which can adversely affect their mental health. The LGBTQIA+ community is often subjected to microaggressions, such as 'Oh, that's so gay' and 'You need to man up.' Since these microaggressions harm people, we should discuss sexual orientation at work openly.

Dependants/caring responsibilities

It is important to understand whether people are caring for children, disabled children, disabled adults or elderly folk. To help people balance their work and home life, the organisation needs to have flexible and agile working policies and practices in place.

National identity

Increasing levels of national consciousness have led to more people expressing their national identity. In the UK, there are a number of national identity categories, including English, Welsh, Scottish, Northern Irish and British. There should be an option for a person to write in their own nationality if a nationality is not listed on the list. Employees' national identities can provide insights into their cultural backgrounds, experiences and perspectives, enriching a company's understanding of them.

Religion

I recommend that, similar to ethnicity, you consult the ONS's categorisation of religions, which it uses as part of its demographic surveys like the census. Major world religions are typically included by the ONS, but you should also include an 'I prefer to use my own term' option to represent less common religions and faiths in our society.

Social mobility

The UK has one of the poorest rates of social mobility in the developed world. This means that people born into low-income families, regardless of their talent or hard work, do not have the same access to opportunities as those in more privileged circumstances. In collaboration with industry and experts such as The Social Mobility Foundation and The Bridge Group, the government developed a set of questions to understand socio-economic backgrounds. Their questions include the occupation that the main household earner held when they were a teenager, the type of school they attended, whether they were eligible for free school meals, and what the highest qualification of their parents or guardian was. These questions aren't perfect. For instance, I have concerns about asking people about their parents' qualifications, which can be exclusionary and triggering – for example, if you grew up in care.

Armed forces

Those who served in the armed forces might face difficulties finding work after leaving the service. They may also face additional challenges in gaining employment if they become disabled while serving.

Quantitative inclusivity data

We have covered a long list of demographic data, but the ability to see patterns, trends and themes in your inclusive culture is equally important, so you must use quantitative data to measure inclusivity.

The importance of EDI at different levels within an organisation should be gauged. As a result of a survey I conducted on one of my clients' businesses, we discovered that employees felt EDI was 'Very important' for the executive team, their line manager and themselves, but was 'Somewhat important' for their immediate team and the wider organisation. We determined that senior leadership and management communicated the importance of EDI well. That had not, however, permeated the immediate team around them, since it was not as important to them as a team as it was to them as individuals. Additionally, we found that EDI was viewed as 'Extremely important' by women, disabled people, colleagues from ethnic minorities, LGBTQIA+ folk, and those experiencing mental health concerns. In spite of this, some employees who had caring responsibilities felt their situation was not a priority for their manager. This provided the opportunity to train managers on being inclusive of parents and caregivers through flexible working practices.

As soon as you understand the importance of EDI at various levels in your organisation, it is essential to know whether people feel that they belong. Offer them statements such as 'I often worry that I don't have much in common with other employees at my company', 'I feel valued and respected by my manager' or 'I am confident that I can continue my career here', and, on a sliding scale, ask them to rate each statement from 'Strongly disagree' to 'Strongly agree'.

As another way of gauging team involvement, you can ask people to choose from the sliding scale of 'I am generally ignored by others' to 'I feel like a core component of my team with real influence over decisions'. Alternatively, you might ask, 'Have you ever experienced disrespectful or prejudicial behaviour because of your identity?' and offer a scale of 'Never' to 'Every day'.

Qualitative inclusivity data

Your employees will be able to provide you with valuable insights and feedback by answering qualitative, open-ended questions. Here are some examples:

- How should senior leaders improve EDI? What advice do you have for them?

- To recruit more diversity within the organisation, what should the business do?

- How can the organisation ensure that everyone is treated fairly and thrives?

- Our company would like to support our employees by setting up networks and ERGs if they're in high demand. What kind of network or group would you be interested in forming?

You can analyse sentiment from these types of questions, as well as determine key themes and topics, which may be incorporated into your strategy or require further analysis and investigation (for example by holding focus groups or conducting one-to-one interviews with employees).

Return on effort and investment data

Retailers often send emails asking if you are likely to recommend them or their product or service to your friends and family when you buy online from them, to calculate their NPS. As a metric, NPS measures customer satisfaction and loyalty. It is widely used in business to assess customer sentiment and forecast growth. You can use the same approach internally within your organisation by calculating your employee NPS (eNPS). On a scale of 0–10, ask your employees how likely they are to recommend your company to friends, family and associates as an inclusive place to work. eNPS can be calculated by subtracting the percentage of Detractors from the percentage of Promoters. The results can be used to create traffic lights. Passives (who scored 7–8) in the amber zone are employees who are moderately satisfied but not enthusiastic, Promoters (who scored 9–10) in the green zone are highly satisfied and likely to recommend, while Detractors (who scored 0–6) in the red zone are dissatisfied and unlikely to recommend. You can also break this down by group; for example, are disabled people less likely to recommend you as an inclusive employer than the overall average or are working parents and caregivers more likely to do so?

Another favourite question of mine is: 'In the next six months, are you considering leaving the organisation because you don't feel respected or like you belong?' Respondents can select from the following options: 'Yes, I am actively looking', 'I am leaving for other reasons', 'I will not be leaving' or, of course, 'Prefer not to say'. Looking at the salaries of those considering leaving your company alongside hiring, onboarding, training and development costs, and productivity loss, you can estimate the cost of attrition, which is useful for EDI business cases. After conducting the survey, we calculated that my client may lose £466,000 over a six-month period as a result of people actively seeking to leave the company. Parents and those with caring responsibilities were the most at risk. Answering this question alone will make it easier for you to secure funding for EDI initiatives, since you will be able to demonstrate ROI.

Best practices

There are a number of things you can do to ensure you are collecting data in a professional, fair and efficient way.

Test, test and test again

Test your survey with a small, diverse group of people before you go public, as you might accidentally make a mistake, such as missing a drop-down field option or using the wrong language. It is best to test with your employee networks, as these colleagues are more familiar with topics like LGBTQIA+, gender identity and disability inclusion. Test with influential stakeholders, such as senior managers or internal communications experts.

Make every question mandatory

People will ignore and skip over questions if you do not do this, and you will have gaps in your data as a result. You must, however, include a 'Prefer not to say' option in your binary questions (drop-down menus, radio buttons, checkboxes, sliding scales etc) so that they may opt out. The free-text fields should be optional so people will not be forced to provide responses. If someone doesn't want to answer, they can leave these blank.

Allow people to share their preferred terminology

On matters such as gender identity, sexuality and ethnicity, it is best to create a list of options, as we discussed earlier in this chapter, but also include an 'I prefer to use my own term' field. By allowing employees to use their own language, you can acknowledge their existence and lived experience, and try to understand what their needs are in the organisation.

This can sometimes invite inappropriate responses. For example, I received responses to a question about sexual orientation for a client that included 'I like to have sex with flowerpots', 'I like to f**k my car' and 'I'm married, I never have sex any more'. Data like that is quite shocking, but it can also indicate the attitudes of people in an organisation and whether they contribute to homophobic behaviour, such as bullying, microaggressions and toxic banter.

Make data collection easy and accessible

Consider the user experience. Are people doing the survey on their phones while commuting to work? Are they doing it on a big screen at their desk in an open-plan office where they are concerned about being overlooked by colleagues? How can factory workers get online access if they do not have computers? Do you need another method of collecting data? Also, make sure your data collection system is accessible to disabled people. As an example, does it support screen readers – assistive technology used by colleagues who are blind or have difficulty seeing? If English is not someone's first language or if they have difficulty reading – for example, they might be dyslexic – make sure you use plain, simple language. If in doubt, ask a digital accessibility expert to conduct a Web Content Accessibility Guidelines (WCAG) audit on the software you intend to use.

Remind people about confidentiality

This needs to be done several times throughout the survey. Make sure people know their data is anonymous and point them to the FAQ document, which should contain privacy, confidentiality and data-sharing details to address any concerns they might have. At the bottom of your survey, include a statement like: 'Data from our survey may be shared with your employer. In such cases, the information provided to them will be anonymised so that the identities of people who have taken part in our survey remain hidden. Your employer will be restricted as to who can see and use the information we provide. Please contact [name and email address] with any questions or concerns.'

How to analyse and report on your findings

It isn't enough to collect the data; you need to analyse it and communicate it to your colleagues and agree on the best ways to use it to adapt and improve your organisation's approach to EDI.

Analysing data

It's important to break down questions by cohorts. Take a sliding scale statement like 'I feel like I belong in the organisation'. The top-line data will likely tell you that most people feel part of the organisation, because you are hearing the voice of the majority, which is misleading. The differences become apparent only when you dig deeper. For example, break down responses by men and women, disabled people versus nondisabled people, or people experiencing racial inequalities.

Don't forget to be aware of bias during data collection. In an EDI survey, people who identify as under-represented are likely to respond because they have a vested interest in it. You may not receive as many responses from colleagues if they do not see themselves as diverse, as we discussed in Chapter One.

Identify themes from your qualitative data and describe each theme in detail. For example, in one client survey, I asked 'What advice would you give senior leaders regarding EDI?' and 'Inclusive Leadership' emerged as a high-level theme. We broke down employee feedback further to find recommendations, including: increase diversity in leadership, promote a genuine commitment to EDI and encourage external visibility of the SLT publicly talking about EDI.

Whenever you create charts like pie charts, bar graphs and line charts etc, make sure that you add narrative to support the charts. For example, in a client's report about employee sexuality, we added the narrative that said, 'As of the last UK census, 89% of respondents identified as straight or heterosexual. Around 1.5 million people (3%) identified as gay, lesbian, bisexual or another sexual orientation (LGB+).[40] According to Stonewall's Rainbow Report, 71% of Gen Z identifies as straight compared to 91% of baby boomers, which could suggest that

LGBTQIA+ inclusion is more important to younger generations than older, more senior leaders.'[41]

Communicating your findings

You should include an executive summary at the top of your report. Senior leaders don't have time to read long reports. They want to know what's important and what needs to be done.

It is important to create different briefing reports for different audiences. The senior executive team will need to know different things than line managers, who need to know different things than your HR business partners.

Completing the feedback loop

You should conduct a workshop with your senior leaders to share feedback on key findings and themes, discuss recommendations and their EDI vision and then create an action plan together. Don't forget, this isn't the sole responsibility of the head of HR.

Because your employees have invested time and emotional energy in sharing their thoughts, feelings and personal information with you, they deserve feedback. It's important to let them know that you have heard them, what you have learned and what you intend to do with the findings.

A useful structure for updating employees is:

1. Give a brief overview of your EDI journey, what you've done so far, and why you did the survey.

2. Evaluate your confidence in the data and response rate.

3. Tell people what is interesting from respondents' demographic data. Don't overwhelm them with too much data – choose what is most interesting.

4. Identify key themes (and if necessary break them down into sub-themes).

5. Tell employees what you're working on and what you've accomplished, because you've probably already begun to make changes and have achieved some quick wins and success.

6. Set expectations by explaining the next steps and plan going forward.

7. Include closing remarks, and thank everyone for participating.

8. Provide your colleagues with a way to provide additional feedback now that they have seen the results. That could be an anonymous feedback form or just an email address.

Artificial intelligence: The exciting future

The future of artificial intelligence (AI) excites me greatly. I am already experimenting with AI to streamline data analysis in EDI. Working with academics and students at the University of Salford, I am developing software and AI that will help clients run EDI surveys on autopilot and provide instant results. In seconds, you can analyse a large data set and generate analysis, results and charts. There are also ways AI can analyse qualitative data and generate instantaneous sentiment and topic or theme analysis. We're going to see more of it, whether we like it or not. As with all these things, AI can be misused and we must be aware of its biases. AI can also help us in positive ways – just look at how it is helping doctors diagnose cancer and treat patients more quickly.

Summary

In this chapter, you have explored the different types of data you can collect in your survey, how to analyse those results, and how to provide feedback to senior leaders and colleagues.

SIX

Plan: Strategising For Equity, Diversity And Inclusion Success

Improving your organisation's approach to EDI should begin with gathering employee data and insights, because understanding the real-life difficulties that employees face allows you to identify specific EDI challenges and take targeted action where it is most needed.

It is also important to do a gap analysis of what you are currently doing with regard to EDI, which is constantly evolving, as this will help you identify any actions that should be added to your EDI strategy in addition to what has already been identified through getting data and insights from your employees.

In this chapter, we will cover the importance of supplementing employee insights with a gap analysis of EDI best practices, setting metrics and key performance indicators, and integrating all of this information into an EDI strategy.

Gap analysis and benchmarking

As part of my work with clients, I use my own gap analysis auditing survey, which I developed based on my first book. I continually refine the survey to ensure it is up to date and contains 100 questions. This survey identifies any areas of EDI best practices the client isn't currently considering and whether they should be integrated into their EDI strategy. Other tools also exist, and I will mention a few examples here. These tools vary in complexity and specialisation with regards to EDI and investment.

Global Diversity, Equity and Inclusion Benchmarks

A great tool to use are the Global Diversity, Equity and Inclusion Benchmarks (GDEIB).[42] This tool is free to use. There are four aspects to the framework:

1. **Foundation**: This drives the strategy, which includes your vision, your leadership responsibility and accountability, and how you structure EDI.

2. **Internal aspect**: This explores how you attract and retain people in your organisation.

3. **External aspect**: This considers both how to listen to and serve the communities you are operating in and the inclusivity of your services, products and marketing.

4. **Bridging**: This connects all aspects to ensure alignment and connection and includes measurement, learning and development, communications and sustainability.

This benchmark gives you a sense of how mature EDI is in your organisation by awarding a level of Inactive, Reactive, Proactive, Progressive or Best Practice Employer.

A particular advantage of the GDEIB is that they are applicable to organisations with global operations. They were designed by a team of EDI experts in collaboration with industry, making them robust.

The National Equality Standard

In 2013, Ernst & Young (now EY) launched the National Equality Standard (NES).[43] This standard was developed 'for businesses by businesses' and provides clear criteria for evaluating EDI. The EDI policies and practices of the organisation are reviewed, areas for improvement are identified, and recommendations are made. The NES was developed and sponsored by EY, supported by the Equality and Human Rights Commission, the Home Office, and the Confederation of British Industry, and developed in partnership with a number of UK and global companies like BT Group, Cisco, Nestlé and Vodafone. The NES has since developed a Global Equality Standard and a Supplier Equality Standard.

The Human Resource Management Diversity and Inclusion Standard

The International Organisation for Standardisation (ISO) created ISO 30415 in 2021, called the Human Resource Management Diversity and Inclusion Standard.[44] This is a useful framework which you can download from the ISO website. As opposed to NES, where the assessors and team support you, you are responsible for self-assessment.

This framework provides guidance and methods for embedding diversity and inclusion in your workplace, such as:

- Demonstrating ongoing commitment to diversity and inclusion

- EDI accountabilities and responsibilities

- Developing an inclusive workplace by valuing diversity

- Assessing EDI objectives, opportunities and risks, as well as actions, measures and outcomes

These are three robust benchmarking models, but organisations may also be interested in other tools. Even though the following standards are not specifically targeted at EDI, they are useful in benchmarking the environmental, social and governance (ESG) agenda, being a good employer and maintaining a sustainable organisation.

B Corp Impact Assessment

An organisation that meets strict social and environmental standards, is transparent and accountable, and has been verified by B Lab is certified as a B Corporation. The B Impact Assessment (BIA) is a comprehensive, well-regarded sustainability benchmarking tool developed by B Corp.[45] EDI is addressed directly in the BIA by a variety of questions and metrics, and companies use it to measure their impact on their workers, community, environment and customers. It includes inquiries about hiring practices, pay equity, diversity among employees and management, and inclusivity at work. It has two sections – Workers and Community.

The Workers section includes the company's contribution to its employees' financial, physical and psychological wellbeing as well as its diversity and inclusion policies and practices. In the Community section, the focus is on the company's impact in the local community and includes diversity and inclusion questions, such as on supplier diversity, community service, and engagement in underserved populations.

It is a robust standard, and although it does not focus solely on EDI, this is woven throughout. It is best to use this standard with the support of EDI experts, since this methodology is not entirely dedicated to inclusion and diversity.

The Responsible Business Map

A not-for-profit organisation called Business in the Community (BITC) developed this standard to help businesses become more responsible.[46] The Responsible Business Map focuses on two aspects – healthy communities and a healthy environment. As part of healthy communities, diversity and inclusion is included along with employment and skills and health and wellbeing.

At the centre of the model, where healthy communities and healthy environments intersect, the healthy business aspect emphasises embedding your purpose, stakeholder collaboration, governance and values. This model is a much lighter version of the BIA from B Corp, and BITC is a fantastic organisation that does excellent work and produces great content that you should follow if your organisation is interested in inclusive growth and an ESG agenda.

Other useful tools

There are numerous other benchmarking tools available that focus on particular diversity demographics. They are good, but, since they are specialised, they do not always take into account the broad spectrum of diversity to help you create your holistic EDI strategy. For example, in collaboration with industry, the Department for Work and Pensions developed the Disability Confident employer scheme, which is free to use. The framework is useful for employers seeking to attract, recruit and retain disabled employees, but it does not consider diversity in its entirety.

When I worked at Deloitte, I enjoyed doing the Working Families Benchmark, which was developed by the charity Working Families – the UK's national charity for working parents and carers.[47] During their annual awards ceremony, they recognise employers that support working families, parents and caregivers well. It is a robust, data-driven benchmark that measures policies and practices for supporting employees with parenting and caring responsibilities.

Finally, there is the UK Workplace Equality Index, a benchmark developed by Stonewall.[48] This index is focused on LGBTQIA+ inclusion, but it is limited for other diversity demographics.

As you can see, there are many benchmarking tools and frameworks available, but, as an HR professional, you should focus on what is important to your people, your leaders and the business, instead of trying to boil the ocean and not land anything.

Go back to the why, how, what

You might feel overwhelmed by the amount of data and information you have at your disposal after you have gathered the data, received input from employee interviews and focus groups, and analysed your existing HR data and the results from benchmarking tools.

Stratifying and interpreting this data will help you develop a future strategy. You need to revisit the whys, hows and whats we highlighted from Simon Sinek's model. The why-how-what approach should shape your strategy document. That means getting back to your why and ensuring your vision is both clear to all members of the organisation and can be clearly and easily articulated. Your strategy should start with this vision.

My client, Electricity North West Limited (ENWL), explain at the beginning of their strategy document how EDI aligns with their people vision, which they say is to 'develop an inclusive culture where colleagues' expertise supports us in future-proofing our network, leading the way to net zero, and always ensuring our customers are at the heart of everything we do'.[49] This can be downloaded from their website.

As well as describing your company's vision, you should describe how EDI aligns with the organisation's values. Provide a definition as well to help people understand how your organisation views EDI.

After you have articulated your why clearly and completely, you can then move on to the how of achieving change. In the next three to five years, you want to take the organisation from your island of now (current state) to your island of the future (future state). The bridge that connects these two islands represents the distinct stages or phases of getting you from one island to the other.

I'll give you two example of clients who have inspired me. A global energy consultancy, specialising in the offshore energy sector and, increasingly, in renewable energy, wanted their organisation to go through three phases:

1. At the **Get-it phase**, everyone understands the importance of EDI and their role in it. People on a logical and rational level understand its importance.

2. In the **Want-it phase**, people want to get involved and do something about EDI. People

connect with the topic on an emotional level and want to see change happen.

3. At the **Capable** phase, people have the skills, tools and capability to bring about the desired change. People feel much more confident in enacting change because they have the skills and tools to make a positive difference.

A professional services client specialising in the built environment, known for its focus on sustainability and community, developed a business strategy. While not specific to EDI, I liked how they presented it. There were several layers, like an onion, as follows:

1. The **foundations of success** layer included building on previous accomplishments. They talked about living their values.

2. EDI wasn't directly mentioned in the next layer – **growing our markets** – but, as we have seen in previous discussions, there is a connection between customers and EDI.

3. The third layer was **culture change**, which has an obvious link to an inclusive culture in the business.

4. To achieve **good growth** (the outer layer of the onion), employees, the company, clients, communities and place must all be aligned.

KPIs and targets

Your strategy may be strengthened by setting targets.
For example, ENWL set targets for gender balance in
their strategy. This was a specific concern for them
as an engineering company in the energy market.
Over five years, they hoped to increase the number
of women on their leadership team from 32% to 37%,
and their number of female engineers from 7% to
12%. This was compared to local market data that
showed 51% of the population of the north-west of
the UK, where ENWL operates, is female. As part
of their data collection plans, they also set a target
requiring at least 80% of their colleagues to share
diversity data with them.

All targets need to be SMART – specific, measurable,
achievable, relevant or realistic to what you are
trying to do and within a specific time frame.[50] To
be realistic, benchmark your targets or contextualise
them based on labour market data or industry
standards.

If you're a company like ENWL and you're looking to
get more women into technical or engineering roles,
you have to deal with the fact that fewer women
graduate with science, technology and engineering
degrees than men, so there is a smaller pool of
candidates you can recruit from.

Using ethnicity data, an employer based in Birmingham or Manchester will have a different demographic to draw on than an employer based in the Bath or North East Somerset region, and census data suggests that businesses based in Brighton and Hove, Manchester, Liverpool or London would have a greater chance of recruiting LGBTQIA+ candidates than in other areas.

Formulate the strategy

You have reiterated your why, identified the how and set targets, if needed. The next step is to figure out the what. Analyse your findings and recommendations, identifying connections or patterns between them, to group them together into what I call 'strategic buckets'.

I worked with a not-for-profit organisation, and following an analysis of an EDI survey, interviews with employees and an auditing and benchmarking process, we created five strategic buckets:

1. Governance and Operations

2. Culture and Leadership

3. Attraction and Recruitment

4. Employee Experience and Processes

5. External Communications and Partnerships

A different set of buckets was created by ENWL, and each bucket had an objective:

- For **Belonging** they said, 'We will work with colleagues to create a great place to work where everyone feels that they belong.'

- For **Talent** they said, 'We will be innovative in attracting talent and making our career paths accessible to the diverse talent in our communities.'

- For **Leadership** they said, 'Our leaders will support all colleagues, driving respect and fairness in everything that we do.'

- For **Community** they said, 'We will champion diversity and inclusion in our communities to drive positive change.'

Another client developed three strategic buckets called Tools and Resources, Capabilities, and Culture.

The key is to create your own strategic buckets, or themes, to make sense of your unique organisation, your unique culture, the industry you are working in, where you are currently at (current state), where you are trying to get to (desired future state) and what feels achievable and realistic for you and your organisation to implement.

Obviously, your EDI strategy has to be unique to your business. You can't just take a cookie-cutter approach to this. The examples above can serve as inspiration, but do not copy them as they might not work for you. Using the data you've collected, you must come up with your own strategic buckets that make sense to you and your organisation.

Having developed these strategic buckets, you then need to fill them up with the actions or activities you intend to take. This is the final layer of Simon Sinek's start-with-why approach (why-how-what). Describe what you will build and deliver; for example, initiatives, interventions, projects, programmes, training, charters, partnerships, specialist benchmarking, awards, policies, process re-engineering, ERGs, forums, further data collection, and feedback.

It is important to have KPIs for each strategic bucket and its activities. Under the Culture bucket, you might run an inclusive leadership development programme, with a KPI of getting 80% of your senior leaders through it by a particular date. As an example, in Chapter Three we discussed Talogy's Perceptions model and using the six leadership cultural competencies as a way to measure the inclusive behaviours of these leaders. To determine whether the scores changed after measuring against this model, you could do a 'before and after' assessment. You might also consider setting binary KPIs, such as 'Have we implemented an initiative or not on time?', and you might audit the accessibility of your careers website against the WCAG standards. The measure for that is whether or not you have conducted the audit by a specific date, severity of issues identified and whether you have or have not created a remediation plan to fix these issues.

This process can feel overwhelming, as, indeed, reading this chapter might feel, since you are trying to make sense of and organise your data and insights. Then you need to put all of that into a framework. This process involves dealing with many collaborators and leaders in the organisation, who may have different views on importance and priorities as you work on it all.

To take the pressure off, I recommend breaking your strategy down into phases. One of my clients divided their planning into three phases: Starting, Maturing and Leading. Starting was centred around getting things moving. During the Maturing phase, they wanted to build on what they had begun, taking it to the next level before reaching the Leading phase. It may help to ease your anxiety if I remind you that EDI is not a sprint, but a marathon.

I was part of the BBC User Experience and Design (UX&D) team, and my manager used the analogy of Ice, Water and Steam to discuss new features. We were actively working on something at the Ice stage – it was well defined, understood and solid. Ideas were almost ready at the Water phase but needed to be refined. Work in the Steam phase was further ahead in time, undefined and needed clarifying and shaping further before we were ready to move forward with it. You do not need to worry about ideas in the Steam phase, way in the future, except when they become Water.

Summary

As a result of following the above process, you will have a robust EDI strategy document. You need to share that strategy document with your key stakeholders – senior leaders, team leaders, ERG network leaders, and employees as a whole. You may wish to communicate publicly, externally.

It is important to keep things simple because if you overcomplicate the process, it will be difficult to implement, as we will discuss in the next chapter. This is a long process, but it is worth it.

SEVEN

Implement

It's unfortunate that I have to write this chapter, but, sadly, it is necessary that I do because so many organisations work through the phases we have discussed in this book and create a beautifully branded strategy document that they don't then implement because other matters take precedence. There could be external factors, such as a global pandemic, a recession, a busy seasonal period (for example, my clients in hospitality and retail are especially busy over the festive period), or internal factors, such as organisational transformation programmes or mergers and acquisitions. Organisations get distracted, lose interest and momentum and forget why they set out on an EDI journey in the first place, which leads to EDI falling down the priority list.

Change management models

Using business models can help you frame your thinking and approach when implementing change in your organisation, which is why I like to work with them. I will introduce you to four I have found useful.

Lewin's Change Management model

There are three phases in Lewin's Change Management model:

1. Unfreeze

2. Change

3. Refreeze[51]

It takes a long time to unfreeze the status quo and ingrained behaviours and norms, and then implement inclusivity changes so that they stick in the refreezing stage. The idea of thinking about change as a series of three distinct phases may be useful, but I feel it is oversimplified for the complexity and multiple strands of EDI.

Kotter's Eight Stages of Change Management model

This is my personal favourite. With this model, you'll get a more thorough and practical framework that goes through eight accelerators of change over three phases to effective change in an organisation:

1. Creating the climate for change

2. Engaging and enabling the organisation

3. Implementing and sustaining change

Phase 1 is to create the right climate of change. To do this, you need to:

- Create a sense of urgency

- Build a guiding coalition

- Form a strategic vision

To create a sense of urgency in an organisation, you have to collect and analyse data that exposes EDI problems as discussed in chapters four and five. The suggestions in chapters two and three can help you build a guiding coalition of senior leaders. Together, they can help you articulate why EDI is so important to your organisation's success.

Phase 2 is about engaging and enabling the organisation, and you need to:

- Enlist an army of volunteers

- Enable action by removing barriers

- Generate short-term wins

For large-scale change to occur, individuals must actively contribute to the cause, while collectively they need to join forces in pursuit of the same goal.

Phase 3 is about embedding the change within the organisation:

- Sustain acceleration
- Institute change

As your credibility grows, you will be able to improve systems, structures and policies. Be relentless with initiating change until the vision of a more equitable, inclusive and diverse organisation becomes a reality. To institute change, you need to explain how new behaviours contribute to an inclusive organisation and make sure they continue until they become strong enough to replace old habits. You should evaluate management practices to ensure that the new behaviours, mindsets and ways of working you adopted are reinforced.[52]

What we've discussed in chapters two through five in this book covers the first phase of John Kotter's model of creating a climate of change within an organisation. Kotter suggests creating urgency within the organisation. Using the collected and analysed data, you can create this sense of urgency by understanding what problems and threats your organisation faces, as well as the costs and risks associated with them. The organisation may face legal or reputational risks if it does not address noninclusive behaviour. You can also identify exciting opportunities for inclusive growth. You should develop a strategic vision for change with an eager SLT and get their buy-in on initiatives that will make the vision a reality.

Within the second and third phases, you can plan for the remaining accelerators:

- Enlist a volunteer army

- Enable action by removing barriers

- Generate short-term wins

- Sustain acceleration

- Institute change

In Phase 2, once the vision is communicated, Kotter suggests enlisting the help of a volunteer army. It is not essential that everyone is enlisted at the beginning. Having just 15% of your workforce on board could be enough to get momentum. As discussed earlier in the book with the Rogers Diffusion Curve, you should identify your innovators and early adopters to reach a tipping point before appealing to your early and late majority. It is crucial that your organisation enables action by identifying and removing any barriers that people may experience when implementing change. To remove barriers, you must first identify them. It can be useful to consider the following:

- Take a moment to reflect on why previous initiatives failed. At what stage did they fail? Did they get off the ground at all? Did they stall in the middle? Were they completed, but then failed to succeed?

- Despite appearing helpful, many commonly accepted statements hinder efforts to overcome legacy obstacles, such as 'That's just how things are done around here' and 'That didn't work before, we won't do it again'.

You should then build momentum by capitalising on short-term wins. People will then feel progress is being made.

In Phase 3, you must sustain acceleration and remain committed to EDI, even after you have achieved early success, when complacency may set in. You have to continue building your volunteer army (bringing in fresh diverse experiences and perspectives), maintaining that sense of urgency and removing barriers to progress.

Last but not least, you need to institute the change. Kotter suggests that you explain the relationship between new behaviours and organisational success, and that you ensure these persist until they become strong enough to replace old habits. Make sure management practices reinforce your new behaviours, mindsets and ways of working by evaluating systems and processes.

The first seven accelerators are about establishing new ways of working. The eighth and final accelerator is to sustain change into the future by ensuring that these new inclusive ways of working are deeply rooted and anchored in the organisation.

Kotter's eight accelerators are useful for implementing EDI as a change movement. When it comes to implementing EDI change, I tend to agree with Gert Bosscher, who says that 'It's not a project. It's a movement. It's a journey. Join us and leave your mark.'[53]

ADKAR model

As Kotter's framework describes the steps to organising change, the ADKAR model, which stands for Awareness, Desire, Knowledge, Ability and Reinforcement, helps to mobilise your people in the following ways:

- **Awareness**: You must make your people aware of the need for change. This means using your CEO's vision statement, which should clearly articulate why the business is invested in EDI and why the change is required. If you have followed the steps set out in this book, you will find this stage straightforward.

- **Desire**: You then need to create a desire so people want to support and get involved in the changes you plan to make. You have to appeal to people's heads and hearts.

- **Knowledge**: Despite wanting to support you and get involved, people need to know how to make a difference. It might be that you say, 'Actually, we want our leaders to behave more inclusively.' People might be willing, but they might not know how to do that. To make the change successful, you need to provide people with the necessary knowledge.

- **Ability**: This comes down to the skills needed along with the knowledge required to implement change in the organisation.

- **Reinforcement**: Finally, you need to reinforce and validate people's involvement to sustain the change.[54]

Maurer's Three Levels of Resistance

In general, people do not like change, so whenever you implement a change, whether it's a new IT system or an EDI strategy, you'll encounter opposition. By using the Maurer framework, you can think about what resistance and objections you might encounter and how to plan ahead to overcome some of those obstacles.[55]

A pyramid is formed by the three levels of the model:

1. **'I don't get it'** is the first level at the base. Here you articulate the rationale and need. This appeals to the logical, rational side of the human brain, which is where you need to present the business case and data we discussed previously. Providing you have the data to support your messaging, this should be a straightforward step.

2. The second level is titled **'I don't like it'**. Because it's an emotional reaction, it's harder to respond to. It's important to remember that people have a fear of saying or doing the wrong thing, and you might have employees who think it's a 'bunch of lefty, woke, political-correctness-gone-mad nonsense'. In other words, you need to determine what needs to be said or done to remove people's fear about the journey you want to take.

3. The third level is **'I don't like you'**. This is the hardest to address. People might not trust you as a leader to implement the change. If they don't believe that you are being authentic about EDI, they might not follow you. The business must talk about EDI authentically and make everyone aware of the great things that will happen if the

business becomes more diverse and inclusive. Will it help us innovate better? Are we able to better serve our clients? Are we able to retain our talent?

I'm trying not to make this chapter boring or overly academic, but it helps us plan implementation if we have some models that we can use to structure our thinking and start applying to our business. As with any model, please use what will work for your organisation, ignore what won't and customise it for your company.

Roadmap to underpin your strategy

We have discussed creating a strategy, but a strategy on its own is not enough because you need to take action and develop a delivery plan that enables it to succeed. You should create a roadmap that includes:

- Your strategic buckets
- Initiative names and objectives sitting inside each bucket
- Breaking these initiatives down further into actions and deliverables per quarter, week or month
- Dependencies between your activities
- Status of your work, such as 'To do', 'Working on it', 'Stuck/delayed' and 'Done'

- Success measures and KPIs

- Required resources

- Issues and risks and how to mitigate them

Covering each strategic bucket, create a responsible, accountable, consulted, informed matrix. Document who is responsible for delivering the work, which individual is ultimately accountable for each strategic bucket, who you will consult with and who you're going to keep up to date and informed.

Now that you've thought about your change management approach and the roadmap that's going to deliver that change, let's talk about budgets and resources because, unfortunately, many organisations say EDI is important, but they do not provide enough funding or resources to achieve the results they desire.

Many people have the misconception that EDI is only available to big companies with deep pockets. Thousands of people are employed by famous companies, such as Google, McKinsey, Deloitte or the BBC, who invest heavily in EDI, but it is possible for any company of any size to invest in EDI because it is all about the culture. Even though my smallest client has only twelve employees, the founder is thinking about the culture of the organisation, client service and business development opportunities. As the business grows and scales, he wants to ensure that it has a positive, inclusive culture. EDI is not just for big companies with big budgets; smaller businesses can also invest in it.

For EDI to succeed, funding must be adequate, otherwise people become frustrated, initiatives fail and EDI leaders burn out due to a lack of support, resources or budget. Each initiative in your roadmap needs a designated sponsor and budget holder who is ultimately accountable for its success; for example, you might have a project to make your careers website accessible by conducting a WCAG audit with an accessibility specialist. This is something your IT department could be responsible for and the money that you spend on doing an accessibility audit should come from their budget.

CASE STUDY: Reed Talent Solutions

Under the leadership of Managing Director Lee Gudgeon, Reed Talent Solutions (RTS) has embraced EDI as not just buzzwords but as the driving force behind their success.

Their journey began with a focus on women in leadership, setting the stage for an inclusive future. RTS saw past quotas and platitudes, evolving into a champion of true belonging for all. From race and ethnicity to disability and age, every voice finds a seat at the table, empowered by strong leadership and championed by executive sponsors like Lee.

'EDI isn't just about getting people in; it's about ensuring they thrive,' Lee emphasises. This dedication to individual success unlocks the collective potential of their diverse workforce. Collaboration becomes the norm, and products and services resonate with a broader market, propelling RTS towards inclusive growth.

In Lee's words, 'We want to be educators, inspiring others to follow our EDI path.'

Summary

In this chapter, you have learned how to implement a sustainable and lasting change strategy, how four change models can help you organise, and what budget and resource commitments you need to achieve success.

EIGHT

Improve And Sustain Change

From Strategy To Action

This is the final step of the Inclusivity Flywheel model. In this chapter, we explore the application of Agile to enhance EDI strategies and enable you to create sustainable change in your organisation. Drawing from my experience at the BBC within UX&D, I demonstrate how Agile's core principles of adaptability, responsiveness and a people-centric focus can revolutionise EDI initiatives, and how it is useful to take inspiration from the Agile scrum methodology that I learned working on technology projects in the UX&D team. We'll delve into practical Agile techniques, such as creating backlogs, running sprints and conducting retrospectives, tailored specifically for EDI goals. This approach not only streamlines the implementation process but also ensures these initiatives remain dynamic and responsive.

Adaptability and responsiveness

EDI roadmaps are typically implemented over a three- to five-year period, but so much can change in that time frame that companies must be flexible and responsive.

The Agile manifesto includes useful values:

- **Individuals and interactions over processes and tools**: The focus of EDI is on people-centred change. When you implement change, keep the people in your organisation foremost in mind, not the processes, systems or tools you'll be using.

- **Working software over comprehensive documentation**: This could be working EDI solutions over comprehensive documentation. As an EDI professional, you need to make sure you do the work, build solutions, test ideas, implement quickly and respond to feedback rather than writing endless papers, documents and business cases.

- **Customer collaboration over contract negotiation**: Instead of wasting time discussing how you will all work together and getting caught up in organisational politics, you want to break down silos within the organisation and work collaboratively with stakeholders. You need to build strong working relationships and collaborate across the organisation to achieve your goals. Trust, openness and honesty are paramount to success.

- **Responding to change over following a plan**: When implementing your EDI strategy, things will happen that steer you off course. Staying flexible and adaptable to change instead of following a rigid plan will be crucial.[56]

Putting Agile into practice

Keeping these Agile values in mind, let's explore the practical application of the Agile methodology as it relates to EDI.

Establish a 'backlog'

Your backlog is like a queue for your work. Your top priority, well-defined work, is at the top of your list. The lower priority, less defined items which will be addressed eventually, are at the bottom. When you are ready to work on a new initiative, start by picking the next item from the top of the backlog. This is a good method of organising your work.

Work in sprints

In sprints, you deliver your work in time-boxed intervals. These intervals normally last three or four weeks and don't change.

Each sprint begins with a planning session where the team decides which high-priority backlog items to tackle, breaks them down into manageable tasks, estimates effort, develops a clear plan for completing the work within the sprint's time frame, and ensures everyone is committed and aligned.

Team members hold daily fifteen-minute check-ins (called 'stand-ups') to talk about what has been accomplished, what is needed today and any issues or roadblocks.

Hold a show-and-tell (or sprint review) at the end of your sprint to demonstrate what you've built. If you're looking at your parental leave policy, for example, you might give a presentation on benchmarking or market analysis and ask for feedback before recommending changes (another presentation in your next sprint).

Use retrospectives

The team gathers for a sprint retrospective to reflect, learn, grow and determine improvements that should be made after a sprint's hard work, highlighting successes and challenges. As the team brainstorm improvements for the next sprint, they focus on process, tools, quality and communication. Everyone is heard, leading to actionable steps and renewed focus.

Sprints, capacity and empowered teams

Because the Agile methodology embraces a sprint-based approach, it empowers you to break work down into smaller, more achievable chunks. This iterative nature makes it easier to allocate resources effectively and ensure tasks align with time-boxed sprint time frames. If a task feels too large, break it down further instead of overloading the sprint. Agile encourages flexibility and continuous improvement – at the end of each sprint cycle, you can evaluate progress, make adjustments and pivot as needed to respond to organisational needs or new information and data. This iterative approach, punctuated by reviews and retrospectives, keeps your EDI initiative on track and responsive to change.

Capacity planning is crucial for sprint success. Consider team members' availability over the two- to four-week sprint duration. Will anyone be on holiday, training or engaged in other projects? Understanding individual capacities prevents overcommitting and ensures realistic goals.

Empowered, diverse teams are at the heart of Agile. Build sprint teams that harness the richness of diverse perspectives and expertise. Imagine IT, HR and marketing professionals working together towards a common EDI goal – this cross-functional collaboration sparks innovation and drives progress.

Agile teams thrive on trust and empowerment. Instead of being micromanaged, specialists are trusted to own their tasks, choose their tools and manage their work independently. This self-organised approach fosters accountability, ownership and high-quality outcomes.

Key roles within Agile teams include:

- **Product owners**: The visionaries and strategists who prioritise EDI goals, maintain the backlog and guide sprint content.

- **Scrum masters** (or consider alternatives like 'scrum coach'): The facilitators who remove roadblocks, encourage communication and coach the team towards continuous improvement. They ensure the Agile framework runs smoothly, tying sprints together for a seamless EDI journey. It is worth noting that the term 'scrum master' has been the subject of considerable debate in recent years. It is intended to refer to mastery of the scrum framework, but it can remind people of slavery and colonialism, which is a painful reminder of oppression and inequality. A number of alternatives have been proposed, such as scrum coach, facilitator, guide, and team lead, which aim to be more inclusive and equitable.

- **The Agile specialists**: The empowered team members, subject matter experts, who tackle challenges head-on and collaborate to deliver impactful EDI outcomes. They self-organise, holding themselves accountable for excellence.

The Game Changer Index

My team and I love to use the Game Changer Index (GC Index®) tool.[57] This innovative instrument is designed to determine your natural inclination towards creating a meaningful impact. Those familiar with DiSC profiling or Myers–Briggs will recognise similarities in the assessment method; however, these conventional tools predominantly examine personality traits, which can be variable depending on the working environment (or, in my experience, even influenced by which side of the bed I get out of!). In contrast, the GC Index specifically evaluates your innate drive to effect change.

The GC Index was conceived in 2012 by Dr John Mervyn Smith and his business partner, Nathan Ott. Their objective was to scientifically pinpoint individuals capable of making a significant impact in the workplace, who they termed 'Game Changers'. During their research, they identified four additional inclinations that characterise how individuals make an impact.

These five proclivities are:

1. **Game Changers**: Visionary thinkers, fuelled by creative innovation and adept at devising novel approaches, they thrive on exploring potential and possibilities.

2. **Strategists**: These individuals provide structure to ideas, prioritising clarity and direction. They focus on understanding the reasons behind actions and crafting effective methods to achieve objectives.

3. **Implementers**: Pragmatic and results-oriented, they are motivated by the completion and delivery of projects. Preferring efficiency over perfection, they are content with achieving an 80% solution.

4. **Polishers**: Dedicated to continuous improvement and quality enhancement, they excel in refining projects from 80% to perfection, striving to create the optimal outcome.

5. **Playmakers**: Central to uniting these diverse inclinations, they foster team consensus and ensure collective efforts are aligned towards a common goal.

The GC Index enables you to identify how you can most effectively contribute to EDI initiatives. For example, if you score highly as an Implementer, you may find your strength lies in executing EDI initiatives rather than in brainstorming or strategic planning. Conversely, if you are more of a Strategist but less of a Playmaker, your focus may be on the purpose and journey of EDI initiatives rather than on uniting the team.

Understanding these five inclinations allows you to leverage your strongest energies, thereby maximising your impact in your professional role.

The GC Index not only aids in identifying your most effective role in driving change but also serves as a powerful tool in discussing diversity amongst business leaders. It allows for a conversation on diversity that extends beyond traditional dimensions like gender, ethnicity, disability and LGBTQIA+ identities. This approach diminishes the anxiety often experienced by senior leaders, offering them a more relatable perspective on the necessity of diversity of thought and energies through the lens of these five inclinations. For instance, a balanced SLT benefits from a mix of creative visionaries (Game Changers), strategic planners (Strategists), action-oriented doers (Implementers), quality drivers (Polishers) and unifying agents (Playmakers).

A business strategy for continuous improvement

We've discussed implementation theory and practice, and now we're going to take a step back and talk about how to sustain change for a longer period of time. Your EDI strategy should eventually become integrated with your overarching organisational strategy so that it is not a stand-alone strategy once you have implemented it. Then it will become a part of your organisation's fabric.

For continuous improvement, you need to go back to data. Data collection shouldn't be a one-off event. You need to continually monitor patterns and trends to determine whether things are improving. You need to keep collecting quantitative metrics; for example, organisational demographic data, inclusive culture data, hiring and promotion rates of different demographics. You should monitor your representation on a regular basis to see if it is improving and changing.

The quantitative data you collect could include:

- **Hiring and promotion rates**: Are men promoted more quickly than women? Are people from an ethnic minority background less likely to get a job offer?

- **Workplace retention or employee turnover levels**: Do working parents or people with caring responsibilities leave the organisation more frequently than others?

- **The number of people participating in EDI initiatives**: Is there a particular cohort of the organisation that you are struggling to engage?

- **Gender pay gaps**: The government requires UK organisations with 250 or more employees to report gender pay gaps. While technically not required under the regulations, many forward-thinking businesses with fewer than 250 employees calculate their gender pay gaps anyway. Some organisations voluntarily calculate and publish other pay gaps, including ethnicity and disability pay gaps. In the future, ethnicity and disability pay gaps may be included in the legislation, although at the time of writing, only gender pay gaps must be reported.

- **Pay ratios**: These measure the difference between your highest- and lowest-paid employees. For example, the median FTSE 100 Index CEO earns 118 times the median UK full-time worker.[58] Is it prudent for employers to prioritise excessive pay rises for senior executives when so many households are struggling with living costs? The way employers distribute the wealth their workforce creates has a big impact on people's living standards, which is why I am a fan of employee-owned businesses such as Turley, Arup and John Lewis Partnership. According to the 'People Powered Growth Report' by the Employee Ownership Association, 'in an economy where official data suggests the majority of business owners are white and male, EOBs [employee and worker owned businesses] put ownership into the hands of diverse groups who typically don't own businesses'.[59]

The following are examples of qualitative data you could collect:

- **Employee feedback**: This can be through employee engagement surveys, the use of tools like InChorus, Culture Shift or Culture Amp.

- **Culture and behaviour observations**: Are your managers noticing a change in behaviour in their teams? Is there more or less respect for one another? Are there fewer microaggressions or less 'banter' at the office or factory floor? Are the managers or leadership team more engaged? How have their behaviours or leadership styles changed?

- **Your reputation as an employer**: Do you have a positive external reputation? Have you received recognition for your EDI efforts? Are you being praised by the trade press for your work? On social media and platforms such as LinkedIn, Indeed and Glassdoor, where employees can provide feedback, are people talking positively about your business?

To ensure consistency and monitoring of key data points over time, you could develop a balanced scorecard to help measure performance beyond traditional financial metrics. It may be helpful to include the following perspectives:

- **Financial**: Can you draw any correlation between EDI and the profitability of your business? Consider the costs and ROIs of implementing various EDI initiatives.

- **Customer**: Measure customer satisfaction scores. Use the NPS we discussed in Chapter Five to identify whether your customers are Detractors, Promoters or Passives.

- **Stakeholder**: Using your suppliers as your stakeholders, monitor whether your supply chain or supplier base is becoming more diverse. Are you working with more small businesses owned by minority groups? What are your shareholders doing to hold your leadership team accountable for EDI initiatives? Are your business unit leaders actively involved in driving change?

- **Internal business process**: How well are your EDI initiatives being integrated into business-as-usual activities? For example, as part of the product development process, is accessibility a standard development practice for any digital products and services you build, or is accessibility a last-minute afterthought? As you have to fix issues retrospectively and maybe deal with reputational damage, focusing on accessibility at the end of a project is more costly and time-consuming.

- **Learning and growth**: Monitor participation in training courses and workshops. Do your career development programmes promote equitable and inclusive participation? Is EDI impacting innovation and creativity?

- **Employee**: Track the demographic changes discussed in previous chapters. Does employee engagement and satisfaction improve? Remember the eNPS from earlier in the book? Are retention rates rising?

- **Leadership and governance**: Monitor the level of commitment your SLT demonstrates to EDI over time, and whether they have EDI goals and are meeting them.

Continuous support and guidance

A lot of organisations invest a great deal of time and effort into developing their strategies but lose momentum when it comes to implementing lasting changes. It is essential to have encouragement, support and guidance along the way.

You have to keep up with the ever-changing world of EDI. Language is continuously evolving, and there are always new best practices, new research and new insights coming out, so it's important to commit to continuous learning. Two of the inclusive leadership behaviours we discussed previously are having a growth mindset and learning orientation.

As the world is rapidly changing, it is important to consult with experts in the EDI field. They have experience working with different organisations and will help you avoid costly, embarrassing mistakes. By using their experience and expertise to create a shortcut for what needs to be done, an expert will help you speed up the process. It is also important to work with experts with lived as well as corporate experience, as they will provide unique perspectives on your organisation and will assist you in navigating your unseen challenges.

It does not help to keep your cards close to your chest when you are on your EDI journey. Collaborating with other organisations is essential in making an impact. While it is imperative to be cautious in many other areas of business and not divulge important, commercially sensitive information, the key to EDI is working together openly and collaboratively with a wide variety of stakeholders to raise the bar in your industry by sharing and learning from best practice. It is also important to engage your diverse range of internal stakeholders, including your employees, your SLT and your ERGs, as well as your external partners, such as your suppliers, customers and clients, and local community groups. Collaborating with your strategic partners could be beneficial, for example, if you outsource your IT or HR help desk to another organisation so that you can assist each other.

Collaborating with your competitors may feel unnatural, but it is essential because the mission must be to level up the entire industry or sector. You cannot do that on your own. If you are a bank, then partner up with other major financial institutions and banks, your regulator and complementary businesses (like your advertising agency). Even if you are a small business like a small web development agency, you could talk to other local businesses about how you can increase employment opportunities for diverse talent for your sector in your local area.

Work with strategic subject matter experts who may be able to assist you with your EDI efforts. For example, if you want to improve disability inclusion in the workplace, you might work with Purple Space, which assists companies in setting up effective disability employee networks. MyPlus, a company specialising in helping businesses recruit and retain disabled graduates, could also be a good option. Those are niche partnerships; if you are interested in achieving sustainability, you might want to partner with, for example, BITC, a charity dedicated to socially responsible businesses.

Celebrating success and positive PR

Your organisation's success needs to be communicated internally and externally once your strategy is making a positive difference. As a result, you will be able to attract diverse talent and create a positive brand within the marketplace for customers and suppliers by improving your employer brand and employee value proposition.

By sharing best practices, you will inspire other organisations in the industry to improve as well. To achieve this, you could do the following:

- Use your PR agency or team to update your existing PR plan to include EDI content and stories. They will have good relationships with industry publications and will easily be able to create content about your success. Your PR team could submit your organisation for relevant awards.

- Depending on your sector, work with your regulator, such as Ofcom in the media and telecommunications industry, because they often care about EDI, and they run events for businesses within the industry that you can participate in. By attending events and publishing articles, you can establish yourself as a thought leader and forward-thinking employer.

- Plan events, round tables or executive forums that bring together business leaders within your industry, or host a breakfast event or lunch at your office to discuss challenges and share best practices.

- Speak at conferences. HR conferences are the obvious choice, since they are interested in EDI, but also consider industry conferences where EDI may not be on the agenda yet.

- Run webinars or online events. Share knowledge on social media.

- You may want to include a page about EDI achievements in your annual report, or you may want to create a separate impact report about EDI and ESG or Corporate Social Responsibility (CSR). This document enables you to promote what you are doing and builds a positive brand by including key metrics, activities, information on what worked, case studies etc.

Summary

In this chapter, you have dived into turning your EDI strategy into reality. You have learned to embrace the Agile methodology's focus on adapting to change rather than following a rigid plan, and you know to use tools like backlogs, sprints and empowered teams to deliver impactful changes. Discovering your natural drive for impact with the GC Index, you have considered how you are energised for making an impact.

Remembering that EDI is a journey, you now appreciate the need to continuously monitor progress with data, feedback and a balanced scorecard, and understand the importance of both celebrating successes like improved retention and employee engagement and sharing your learnings with the world through PR, events and thought leadership.

Conclusion

The journey to implement EDI change in your organisation is not an easy one. It is my hope that this book has made the path clearer to you and provided you with confidence on how to proceed and accelerate your progress. To give you a practical framework to implement your EDI strategy, I created the Inclusivity Flywheel as the basis for the chapters in this book.

In my experience, implementing EDI changes within an organisation can be challenging and frustrating. All of your hard work will feel worthwhile when you feel traction and see the Flywheel keep spinning, when you see and hear a positive shift in your inclusive culture, and when more and more colleagues realise the importance of EDI and support you in your endeavours. When a colleague tells you that your efforts have made a profound impact on their life, it is especially heartening. They might have previously received lots of job application rejections because of a particular characteristic or circumstance but were able to gain meaningful employment, financial independence and a real sense of purpose because of your fight for change. Then you know your work is invaluable.

Please connect with me on LinkedIn (where I regularly publish interesting content) or get in touch through our website if you would like to learn more about how my team can help you brainstorm ideas, develop your strategy, implement a more inclusive culture in your organisation, improve what you are already doing or build consensus among your critical stakeholders.

Appendix

Scorecard

Answer each of the following questions yes or no to help you determine where you should focus your efforts:

1. Do you have a clearly defined EDI vision statement?

2. Are you regularly holding events or workshops to raise awareness of different lived experiences?

3. Are you encouraging open conversations about EDI in your organisation?

4. Have you communicated the importance of EDI initiatives to your SLT and ensured they understand their vital role in championing them?

5. Are your SLT trained or supported to address common hurdles like fear of missteps, unconscious bias and imposter syndrome?

6. Does your organisation cultivate a culture of psychological safety that allows for open communication, vulnerability and constructive conflict around EDI topics, especially for under-represented voices?

7. Does your organisation go beyond regulatory compliance and industry standards to embrace diversity?

8. Is your organisation actively developing inclusive leadership skills?

9. Do your EDI initiatives actively involve and empower employees to participate across all levels and departments?

10. Are you actively searching for hidden trends and patterns in your data analysis beyond legal requirements and targets?

11. Is your data collection process effective at identifying specific challenges and guiding actionable steps to enhance inclusivity across diverse employee groups?

12. When it comes to the collection and analysis of data, have you successfully addressed employee concerns about privacy and anonymity?

13. In terms of workforce demographics, does your organisation accurately represent the communities and clients it serves and the diversity of talent pools you can draw from?

14. Do you collect diversity data based on factors such as gender identity, ethnicity, disability and social mobility – and, ideally, more characteristics than these?

15. Are you using qualitative and quantitative data to identify trends and gain insights into employee perspectives?

16. To identify areas where EDI strategy can be improved, does your organisation conduct a comprehensive gap analysis against best practices?

17. To evaluate your organisation's EDI efforts, do you use established benchmarking tools?

18. Does your EDI strategy align with and support the overall vision and values of your organisation?

19. Does your organisation have a clear plan for implementing and sustaining its EDI strategy?

20. Are change management models like Kotter's Eight Stages or the ADKAR model used to facilitate the implementation of EDI initiatives?

21. Does your organisation allocate adequate resources and budget to support the successful implementation of its EDI strategy?

22. Does your organisation use Agile methodologies, such as sprints and retrospectives, to implement and manage EDI initiatives?

23. Do you have a system for continuously monitoring and improving EDI efforts and KPIs?

24. Does your organisation integrate EDI strategies into its larger business plan?

For every yes, give yourself one point, and use the following guidelines to interpret your scores:

- If you scored 0–6, this means you are in the Starting level. Don't let this discourage you, however, as it represents a great deal of opportunity for you. It could be the start of a fantastic EDI strategy.

- If you scored 7–18, you're at the Maturing level. Create an action plan for implementing the best practices in this book that will help you become a leading organisation. Make sure you get the help you need to accelerate your efforts so you can achieve your goals.

- If you scored 19–24, then you are at the Leading level – congratulations. It is important that you reflect on what is going especially well and is delivering the greatest impact and double down on these efforts. In addition, you should assess whether any of the recommendations in this book will help you improve even further. Being a leading organisation means you should be sharing your knowledge and best practices with strategic and industry partners.

Notes

1. T Mildon, *Inclusive Growth: Future-proof your business by creating a diverse workplace* (Rethink Press, 2020)
2. T Carmichael and R Rijamampianina, 'A pragmatic and holistic approach to managing diversity', *Problems and Perspectives in Management*, 3/1 (2005), 109–117, www.researchgate .net/publication/233843900_A_Pragmatic_and_Holistic _Approach_to_Managing_Diversity, accessed 29 February 2024
3. F Menzies, 'Inclusion fundamentals: How to foster work settings where employees feel respected', LinkedIn Blog (11 November 2018), www.linkedin.com/pulse/inclusion -fundamentals-how-foster-worksettings-where-menzies -fca, accessed 30 April 2024
4. P Barnet, 'If what gets measured gets managed, measuring the wrong thing matters', *Corporate Finance Review* (2015), https://static.store.tax.thomsonreuters.com/static /relatedresource/CMJ--15-01%20sample-article.pdf, accessed 29 February 2024
5. N Nanji, Z Conway and E Layhe, 'McDonald's workers speak out over sexual abuse claims' (BBC News, 18 July 2023), www.bbc.co.uk/news/business-65388445, accessed 1 November 2023
6. S Bond, 'Uber to pay $4.4 million to employees who were sexually harassed at work' (NPR, 19 December 2019), www

.npr.org/2019/12/19/789949239/uber-to-pay-4–4-million-to
-employees-who-were-sexually-harassed-at-work, accessed
5 February 2024

7. K Makortoff and R Davies, 'Former BrewDog staff accuse craft
beer firm of culture of fear', *The Guardian* (10 June 2021),
www.theguardian.com/business/2021/jun/10/brewdog
-staff-craft-beer-firm-letter, accessed 1 November 2023

8. S West, 'H&M faced backlash over its "monkey" sweatshirt ad.
It isn't the company's only controversy', *Washington Post*
(19 January 2018), www.washingtonpost.com/news/arts
-and-entertainment/wp/2018/01/19/hm-faced-backlash
-over-its-monkey-sweatshirt-ad-it-isnt-the-companys-only
-controversy, accessed 1 November 2023

9. E Larson, 'New research: diversity + inclusion = better decision
making at work' (*Forbes*, 21 September 2017), www
.forbes.com/sites/eriklarson/2017/09/21/new-research
-diversity-inclusion-better-decision-making-at-work/?sh=
5894a1ba4cbf, accessed 1 November 2023

10. S Dixon-Fyle et al, *Diversity Matters Even More: The case
for holistic impact* (McKinsey, 5 December 2023), www
.mckinsey.com/featured-insights/diversity-and-inclusion
/diversity-matters-even-more-the-case-for-holistic-impact,
accessed 5 February 2024

11. S Dixon-Fyle et al, *Diversity Wins: How inclusion matters*
(McKinsey, 19 May 2020), www.mckinsey.com/featured
-insights/diversity-and-inclusion/diversity-wins-how
-inclusion-matters, accessed 5 February 2024

12. V Hunt et al, *Delivering Through Diversity* (McKinsey, 18
January 2018), www.mckinsey.com/capabilities/people
-and-organizational-performance/our-insights/delivering
-through-diversity, accessed 1 November 2023

13. V Hunt, D Layton and S Prince, *Why Diversity Matters*
(McKinsey, 1 January 2015), www.mckinsey.com
/capabilities/people-and-organizational-performance/our
-insights/why-diversity-matters, accessed 1 November
2023

14. S Page, *The Difference: How the power of diversity creates better
groups, firms, schools, and societies* (Princeton University
Press, 2008)

15. P Cheese and T Mildon, 'Diversity and inclusion as the
golden thread' (The Inclusive Growth Show, 2020), https://

inclusivegrowthshow.buzzsprout.com/1728737/8108072, accessed 1 November 2023

16. TomboyX, 'Our values' (no date), https://tomboyx.com/pages /community-1, accessed 5 February 2024

17. Sea Change CoLab, 'Purple flag moment: addressing harm and creating safer spaces at work' (no date), https:// seachangecolab.com/purple-flag-moment, accessed 5 February 2024

18. M Brown, Dr, 'The matrix of domination and the four domains of power' (Black Feminisms, 2020), https:// blackfeminisms.com/matrix/, accessed 5 February 2024

19. S Covey, *The 7 Habits of Highly Effective People* (Simon & Schuster UK, Reissue Edition, 19 May 2020)

20. T Van Bommel, PhD, K Robotham, PhD, D Jackson, PhD, *Words Aren't Enough: The risks of performative policies* (Catalyst, 2020), www.catalyst.org/reports/risks -performative-policies, accessed 29 February 2024

21. T Mildon, 'When words are not enough' (The Inclusive Growth Show, 2023), https://inclusivegrowthshow .buzzsprout.com/1728737/12108735, accessed 29 February 2024

22. K Miller, 'The triple bottom line: what it is and why it's important' (Harvard Business School Online, 8 December 2020), https://online.hbs.edu/blog/post/what-is-the-triple -bottom-line, accessed 1 March 2024

23. University of Minnesota, 'Daring to be vulnerable with Brené Brown' (Taking Charge of your Wellbeing, no date), www .takingcharge.csh.umn.edu/daring-be-vulnerable-brene -brown, accessed 5 February 2024

24. NeuroLeadership Institute, 'The 5 biggest biases that affect decision-making' (1 August 2023), https://neuroleadership .com/your-brain-at-work/seeds-model-biases-affect -decision-making, accessed 7 November 2023

25. Harvard, 'About the IAT' (Project Implicit, 2011), https:// implicit.harvard.edu/implicit/iatdetails.html, accessed 7 November 2023

26. Boston University, 'Diffusion of innovation theory' (Behavioral Change Models, 2022), https://sphweb.bumc .bu.edu/otlt/mph-modules/sb/behavioralchangetheories /behavioralchangetheories4.html, accessed 7 November 2023

27. The GC Index, 'Are relationships the key to business success?' (The GC Index News and Blogs, no date), www.thegcindex .com/are-relationships-the-key-to-success, accessed 7 November 2023

28. The de Bono Group, 'Six Thinking Hats' (no date), www .debonogroup.com/services/core-programs/six-thinking -hats, accessed 7 November 2023

29. B Brown, 'Brené Brown and Barrett Guillen on Building Brave Spaces' (17 November 2022), https://brenebrown.com /podcast/building-brave-spaces, accessed 27 March 2024

30. P Lencioni, *The Five Dysfunctions of a Team: A leadership fable* (Jossey-Bass, 2022)

31. S Sinek, *Start With Why: How great leaders inspire everyone to take action* (Penguin, 2011)

32. R Pojasek, 'Asking "why?" five times', *Environmental Quality Management*, 10/1 (2000), 79–84, https://faculty.washington .edu/rsmcpher/Class%20Cases%20and%20Assignments /5%20Whys.pdf, accessed 1 November 2023

33. Talogy, 'Work effectively with anyone using the Talogy Perceptions assessment' (no date), www.talogy.com/en -gb/talent-management-solutions/assessments/talogy -perceptions-inclusive-behaviours, accessed 13 November 2023

34. J Bourke, 'The six signature traits of inclusive leadership: thriving in a diverse new world' (Deloitte Insights, 14 April 2016), www2.deloitte.com/us/en/insights/topics/talent /six-signature-traits-of-inclusive-leadership.html, accessed 1 November 2013

35. N Crowther, 'Nothing without us or nothing about us?' (The Disability Archive, University of Leeds, 2007), https:// disability-studies.leeds.ac.uk/wp-content/uploads/sites/40 /library/crowther-Nothing-without-us-bt.pdf, accessed 19 March 2024

36. Bird & Bird, *Equality, Diversity and Inclusivity Monitoring: A multi-country guide* (HR Data Essentials, May 2022), www.twobirds.com/en/hr-data-essentials/international -perspectives/articles/equality-diversity-and-inclusivity -monitoring, accessed 1 March 2024

37. Stonewall, 'List of LGBTQ+ terms' (no date), www.stonewall .org.uk/list-lgbtq-terms, accessed 22 November 2023

38. The Washington Group on Disability Statistics, 'Labor force survey disability module (LFS-DM)' (no date), www

.washingtongroup-disability.com/question-sets/wg-ilo
-labor-force-survey-disability-module-lfs-dm, accessed 22
November 2023

39. Stonewall, 'List of LGBTQ+ terms' (no date), www.stonewall
    .org.uk/list-lgbtq-terms, accessed 22 November 2023

40. C Barton, '2021 census: what do we know about the LGBT+
    population?' (UK Parliament House of Commons Library,
    16 January 2023), https://commonslibrary.parliament.uk
    /2021-census-what-do-we-know-about-the-lgbt-population,
    accessed 30 January 2024

41. C Billson, 'Younger Brits more queer than ever before,
    eye-opening Stonewall study finds', *Pink News* (6 October
    2022), www.thepinknews.com/2022/10/06/younger-brits
    -more-queer-than-ever-before-eye-opening-stonewall-
    study-finds, accessed 23 November 2023

42. D&I Leaders, 'The Global Diversity, Equity & Inclusion
    Benchmarks' (no date), https://dileaders.com/gdeib,
    accessed 2 December 2023

43. National Equality Standard, 'National Equality Standard
    (NES)' (no date), www.nationalequalitystandard.com
    /national-equality-standard, accessed 1 March 2024

44. International Organisation for Standardisation, 'ISO
    30415:2021(en) Human resource management: diversity
    and inclusion' (2021), www.iso.org/obp/ui/#iso:std:iso:
    30415:ed-1:v1:en, accessed 2 December 2023

45. B Lab UK, 'What is a B Corp?' (no date), https://bcorporation
    .uk/b-corp-certification/what-is-a-b-corp, accessed 2
    December 2023

46. Business in the Community, 'The responsible business map'
    (no date), www.bitc.org.uk/the-responsible-business-map,
    accessed 1 March 2024

47. Working Families, 'The Working Families Benchmark'
    (no date), https://workingfamilies.org.uk/employers
    /benchmark, accessed 2 December 2023

48. Stonewall, 'UK Workplace Equality Index' (no date), www
    .stonewall.org.uk/build-workplace-works-lgbtq-people/uk
    -workplace-equality-index, accessed 2 December 2023

49. Electricity North West, 'Diversity and inclusion' (no date),
    www.enwl.co.uk/about-us/careers/diversity-and-
    inclusion, accessed 2 December 2023

50. Mind Tools, 'SMART goals: how to make your goals achievable' (no date), www.mindtools.com/a4wol18/smart -goals, accessed 2 December 2023

51. S Hussein et al, 'Kurt Lewin's Change model: a critical review of the role of leadership and employee involvement in organizational change', *Journal of Innovation and Knowledge,* 3/3 (September–December 2018), 123–127, https:// doi.org/10.1016/j.jik.2016.07.002

52. Kotter, 'The 8 Steps for Leading Change' (no date), www .kotterinc.com/methodology/8-steps, accessed 6 November 2023

53. Kotter, 'The 8 Steps for Leading Change' (no date), www .kotterinc.com/methodology/8-steps, accessed 6 November 2023

54. Prosci, 'The Prosci ADKAR Model' (no date), www.prosci .com/methodology/adkar, accessed 6 February 2024

55. J Reiling, 'Maurer 3 Levels of Resistance and strategic project management' (The Strategic Project Manager, 10 May 2022), https://bethestrategicpm.com/the-maurer-3-levels-of -resistance-and-strategic-project-management, accessed 6 February 2024

56. M Beedle et al, 'Manifesto for Agile Software Development' (Agile Manifesto, 2001), https://agilemanifesto.org, accessed 1 February 2024

57. The GC Index, 'Why the GC Index®' (no date), www .thegcindex.com/why-the-gc-index, accessed 6 February 2024

58. Green World, 'Calls for maximum 10:1 pay ratio as average CEO wages rise' (22 August 2023), https://greenworld .org.uk/article/calls-maximum-101-pay-ratio-average-ceo -wages-rise, accessed 22 February 2024

59. EO Knowledge Programme, *People Powered Growth: The rapid and impactful rise of employee and worker ownership in the UK* (Employee Ownership Association, 2023), https:// employeeownership.co.uk/common/Uploaded%20files /EO-Knowledge-Programme-Report-2023.pdf, accessed 22 February 2024

Acknowledgements

I am grateful to my former managers who have been exceptionally inclusive and empowered me to achieve my best. They have taught me a great deal about being an inclusive leader, and this book is based on what I have learned from them.

I want to thank all of the clients I have worked with since running my own consultancy practice for putting their trust in me to help them build an inclusive workplace that they can be proud of. Working with all of my clients has been a wonderful experience for me, and I have gained just as much from them as they have from me.

I would like to thank my team – Brooklyn, Giverny and Luis – for the amazing job they're doing supporting our clients and enabling us to achieve our mission to help organisations become thriving, inclusive workplaces that allow everyone to excel.

My thanks go out to Siobhan and everyone at Rethink Press for helping me get my knowledge and experience out of my head and into your hands.

I would like to thank my fabulous clients and colleagues – Caroline G, Chrysta P, Devi V, Rachel C, Sharon A and Tracey H – for reviewing my manuscript before it went to print and sharing their HR and EDI expertise and knowledge with me to make sure this book is accurate, practical, helpful and relevant for you.

I'd like to thank my team of personal care assistants who are incredibly dedicated and reliable for helping me live an independent life, which includes supporting me to work so I can give my clients my best.

I would like to give a hug and huge thank you to my boyfriend, Chris, for all of his support and encouragement in my work.

The Author

 Toby Mildon is a pioneering EDI architect and the founder of Mildon, a consultancy dedicated to transforming workplace cultures. His expertise is rooted in his notable tenures at the BBC, Deloitte and Accenture, where he honed his skills in promoting EDI.

Toby's work extends beyond consultancy, as he is a celebrated author and speaker. His first book – *Inclusive Growth* – encapsulates his innovative model for integrating EDI in corporate structures and is a testament to his deep understanding of the field. His thought leadership articles appear in publications such as *People Management*, *HR Review*, *HR*, *The Daily Telegraph* and literature from the British Computer Society. He has also contributed to other authors' books, including *Where Is My Office?* by Chris Kane and Eugenia Anastassiou and *The Human Workplace* by Andy Swann.

As a respected influencer, Toby's insights are widely sought after for driving cultural change in the workplace. His approach is action-centred, focusing on tangible strategies to cultivate equitable, inclusive and diverse environments. His influence is evident in the way professionals and organisations are re-evaluating their approach to embracing inclusivity.

The focus of Toby's work is not just on changing the narrative around EDI but also on creating actionable pathways for organisations to deeply embed these values. He is a catalyst for positive change in today's corporate world, as his work signifies a shift towards more equitable, diverse and inclusive workplaces.

Visit Toby's website:

🌐 www.mildon.co.uk.

Listen to the podcast where Toby interviews EDI experts and business leaders who are making a difference:

🎤 https://inclusivegrowthshow.buzzsprout.com.

Connect with Toby on LinkedIn at:

🔗 www.linkedin.com/in/tobymildon.